Abraham

The man who dared to believe God

By
Paul Smith

MOORLEY'S Print & Publishing

ISBN 10: 0-86071-598-1
ISBN 13: 978-086071-598-6

© Copyright 2006 Paul Smith and Headway

All rights reserved. No part of this publication may be reproduced, stored in a retrieval system, or transmitted, in any form or by any means, electronic, mechanical, photocopying, recording or otherwise, without the prior written permission of the publishers.

British Library Cataloguing in Publication Data.
A catalogue record for this book is available from the British Library.

HEADLINE SPECIALS

are published for Headway by

23 Park Rd., Ilkeston, Derbys DE7 5DA
Tel/Fax: (0115) 932 0643

Preface

This little book has been prepared in the hope that it will give a clearer understanding of Abraham's life and faith. You can use it on your own, as part of your devotional programme, or in a house group or study group where you might want to take a different passage each time you meet and gradually work your way through this great story.

Instead of providing different discussion questions at the end of each study you will find, at the back of the book, a list a questions which can be used on each occasion. They are offered in the hope that they will help you understand the story and discover its message for our lives today.

Knowing the story is one thing. Living the truth you discover is another matter. So with this book comes the prayer that you, like Abraham, may discover a faith which dares to believe God's promises and finds Him to be a God who keeps his word.

Introduction

It is virtually impossible to overestimate the importance of Abraham's life and faith. The writer of Genesis gives us an insight into his genealogy (Genesis 11: 27ff), and as the story unfolds we see that he became, in fulfilment of God's promise, not only the leader of a people, but the father of a nation. As we are introduced to God's character and nature in the pages of Scripture He is identified as the God of Abraham, Isaac and Jacob.

Through Abraham the Jewish nation came to birth, and the Jewish religion, though refined later, finds its origin in this man's understanding of God. Both Islam and Christianity, born out of Judaism, look back to Abraham as a founding father. Here we have someone whose importance is acknowledged in three major world religions.

Whilst the Biblical writers may acknowledge various qualities which Abraham possessed, it is his distinctive faith which marks him out. When the writer of the Epistle to the Hebrews invites us to remember the great people of faith, Abraham is given a prominent position. Many of the others merit little more than a verse, but Abraham gets two paragraphs. In this one life, maybe more than any other Old Testament character, we catch a glimpse into the nature of faith. It is this understanding which is crucial if ever we are going to grasp what it is to be a Christian. When Paul wrestles with justification by faith in his Epistle to the Romans, and searches for an Old Testament example, it is Abraham he lays before us. Abraham's faith was counted, reckoned to him as righteousness (Romans 4: 3).

Here we are dealing, not just with a great historical character from whom we can learn many lessons, but someone whose understanding of God and His relationship with human beings is fundamental to everything that follows. No wonder Abraham is called 'the man of faith'.

God takes the initiative
(Genesis 12:1–9)

Even though we have been introduced to Abram through his genealogy at the end of Genesis 11, his story begins in detail with the opening of chapter 12. He belonged to a family of semi nomads who wandered from place to place with their flocks and herds, seeking pasture, staying for a while and then moving on to fresh grazing. By the time Genesis 12 begins, Abram's family group has already travelled many hundreds of miles. Their journey, we are told, begins in Ur of the Chaldeans in what today we would call Iraq. Looking at the map it is easy to understand how the journey to Haran followed the route of the River Euphrates which would have provided water for this travelling group on their journey. Abram's father, Terah, died in Haran, and it is there that we find Abram as chapter 12 begins.

In a real sense Genesis 12 marks a fresh start. The first eleven chapters contain three major stories – creation, Noah and the flood, and the building of the tower of Babel. Things have gone seriously wrong from God's point of view. Human rebellion following creation resulted in human kind being banished from Eden. Universal rebellion resulted in the flood, with only Noah and his family saved. The tower of Babel had been built in a vain attempt to reach to the status that God occupies, and had resulted in the confusion of diverse languages. In just eleven chapters God has spoken three times in judgment. Whilst Genesis 1–11 is not all bad news, predominantly these chapters convey a strong note of human rebellion and Divine displeasure.

As chapter 12 begins this offended God takes another gracious initiative. It comes in the form of a call to an individual. We are not told why God chose Abram, but simply presented with the fact. It was God's initiative, and it was gracious. It was not because Abram was any better than any other person, or because there was anything in Abram which should make God choose him. The origin and motive for the choice lay in God alone. He had a purpose, and He chose Abram as the one through whom it would be worked out.

We cannot escape the doctrine of election. Many Christians today find this uncomfortable. They are filled with questions. Why should God choose one and not another? Why should it be Abram? What was there about Abram that caused God to choose him in this way? These questions, and many like them, have exercised Christian minds for twenty centuries. So we ought not to be surprised that we cannot answer them adequately. If there was an easy answer someone would have discovered it long ago. We simply need to bow before the wonder of it. Election is not, of course, the whole truth, but we cannot deny its presence in the biblical revelation. God does take the initiative. God does choose. God does work out His purpose in people's lives, sometimes because of them and sometimes despite them. As we reflect on our own lives we marvel at the way in which He has guided and directed, often when we were quite unaware of it. The God of Abram is our God too.

The call of God which comes to Abram is profoundly disturbing. He is to leave his country. We may feel that simply to move on is not so challenging for someone who was travelling all the time, but here it is the stability of his own country that he is to leave, and the physical and relational trappings on which he has come to rely. He is given no directions for the journey, save to say that the way will be made plain to him, as it were, a step at a time, for God says, 'I will show you' (12:1).

If, as the biblical writers suggest, Abram's life is to be a model for the faith of all God's people, this is crucially important. It suggests that faith is far more about travelling than arriving. It concerns leaving our comfort zones and security; taking the risk of being obedient to God when we have no proof that God is going to keep His side of the bargain. The call of Abram seems incompatible with a faith that clings on to security; that is not prepared to do new things, and explore new ways of thinking. This is not about stability. This is about adventure.

The instruction concerns a land. The journey will have a destination. He is to travel by faith, but he will know when he has arrived. There is nothing nebulous here. Land is physical. It has boundaries, geography and, one presumes, inhabitants. It will need to be possessed, cultivated, and subdued. So, within the promise of a land God implicitly promises all that is required to make the land his own. God is committing Himself to a programme, to be worked out through Abram, which can be measured.

How different this is to the blessings that we sometimes seek from God. They are far more nebulous and intangible, as though just to make us feel better is the best that God can do. But here it is far more down to earth, far more practical. God promises to bless with real things in a real world.

The promise concerns not only a land, but what God will make of Abram. You will notice that verses 2 and 3 are printed in many Bibles as verse. You will also notice that God makes the promise unconditionally. God says, 'I will do this'. And, of course, when we think about the detail, we see how unlikely, from a human point of view, it is that this promise will be fulfilled. A backward look to Genesis 11: 30 reminds us that Sarai, his wife, was barren. Yet God speaks into that apparently hopeless situation with an unconditional promise. In fact, as we shall see later, the biggest obstacle to the promise being fulfilled becomes the very thing through which God demonstrates His power.

The blessing which God promises appears impossible, but God has given His word. He will do it. Not only will Abram be blessed as God fulfils His promise, but that blessing will overflow to others until all the peoples on earth are blessed through what God does for Abram. With hindsight we marvel at the way in which the promise has been fulfilled. The tone is set for the revelation of God which will be unveiled in the remainder of scripture. Abram learns a lesson which is significant for us all; God blesses in order that we might bless others.

So here we have the command, "Leave your country", and the promise is, "I will make you into a great nation". Of course such a promise requires a response, not in word alone, but in action. Obedience involves far more than saying the right things. We can all do that and remain as we are. No, Abram left (12:4), offering his whole life, and that of all his travelling companions, to God as he ventured forth. We do not know exactly how big this party was. Some are named, but it would be wrong to limit the numbers just to these people. It is far more likely that by this time Abram had become the head of a clan or tribe of people numbering several hundred. We know from Genesis 14:14 that by that time he could muster 318 trained men. It must have been a significant procession leaving for the land which God had promised.

Faith is a risky business, certainly from a human point of view. Some would call it foolhardy or reckless. Some would criticize him for putting the lives of so many in peril. Their criticism indicates that they have never really grasped what faith is all about. Abraham was beginning to discover it. It certainly is not about feelings. Rather, he was discovering that at its heart there lies a reckless abandon to the command and promise of God. No proof. No signed documents on which we can act if things go wrong. Just a sure, confident trust that takes God at His word and dares to believe that He will keep it, no matter what. No wonder the New Testament writers point us back to the patriarch so often. It is here that we discover what faith in God really means. It was this faith, Paul tells us, which was credited to him as righteousness (Rom 4:3).

After some 400 miles they come to the Jordan Valley and Abram, together with his travelling companions, enter it and begin to explore. It is when they reach Shechem, almost 20 miles west of the Jordan River that God once again searches Abram out. The promise made so long ago and so far away is renewed. At last Abram had arrived in the land of promise. This was it. He had been obedient and God had kept His word. They were there. No wonder Abram built an altar. His heart was reaching out to a faithful God and he just had to worship Him.

The pattern is beginning to emerge. God calls, God promises, Abram responds in obedience, God guides on the journey of faith, and there are moments when God comes in a special way to renew His promise. They are moments of encounter. The next stage in the journey is possible because once again God has sought him out.

So on he goes, eventually establishing camp between Bethel and Ai. The travellers could settle, at least for a while. And once again an altar is built, worship is offered and God is sought. Before long he is travelling again, this time south to the Negev. But for a little while he can rest in the land, as he had rested in the promise on the journey.

Tents and altars offer a way of reflecting on the story. In a way they both represent a dimension of Abram's faith. There is a rhythm here. The journeying is punctuated by the camp. The camp is no sooner erected than an altar is built. On all the journey God is the point of reference by which the route is determined and when the camp is established the altar helps everyone get their bearings again.

Tents are portable, offering enough protection to enable the rest of the journey to be undertaken but not enough comfort to make you want to stay there for ever. All that Abram had went with him, because all that Abram had was offered in responsive faith.

Altars are different. They point to God, enabling folk to reach out for Him. They are about worship and sacrifice. And they are permanent. When the tents have gone on, the altars remain. So time and again in scripture we find that places are identified by the altars which have been built there. Sometimes those who have built the altars return to them and offer worship there again, as Abram will do before long. They are a lasting reminder that those who passed this way, on a journey to which God had called them, were folk who took God seriously. The altars invite all who follow on that route to do the same knowing that no matter how risky it may be God always keeps his promises.

Our journey has its tents and altars too. Like Abram we are all on the move. As the hymn writer taught us to sing: "We nightly pitch our moving tent a day's march nearer home". There is a danger that we put our roots down too deep, regarding as permanent what is essentially temporary, only to be disappointed when things pass away. But, if our walk with God is real, we build our altars too. They are the moments of deep encounter, the times when new sacrifices are offered to the God who guides on the journey. Whilst God travels with us all the way, the journey is punctuated by the special encounter, the time of worship deeper and more challenging than the norm. Whilst our tents, like our lives move on and eventually move off, the altars remain, at least for a while. They remind others who travel on the same route after us that before they got there we had met with God on the journey. Thank God for the altars which others have left for us, where we too can worship. May God so encounter us on the journey that new sacrifice and deeper worship may leave a worthy legacy for those who follow.

When things go wrong
(Genesis 12:10-13:4)

It was Abram's exploration of the land which led him south to the Negev, and it was there that famine struck. He was on a journey of discovery, but he was learning about far more than the geography of the land. He was discovering more and more about the life of faith. And here is another lesson which we all need to learn – to be in the place which God has promised is not to be exempt from suffering. It was in that very place that the suffering came.

We all need to learn that lesson. Wherever did we get the idea that to be in the place of God's appointment is to be comfortable? So often the opposite is true. The high moments of religious experience are often followed by times of great testing. Elijah had a time of great victory over the prophets of Baal on Mount Carmel. God was real. Prayer was answered. The fire fell. But before long he was being pursued by an angry queen, plunged into depression and feeling desperately lonely. It was following His baptism, when the Holy Spirit had descended, that Jesus suffered what we have come to call the temptations. To be in the place of blessing is not to be exempt from trial. It is often the very place where trial is just around the corner.

Of course, the most important thing is how we respond to the trials which come. It is, so often, our response which determines the subsequent blessing which God is able to give. In just one verse (v10) we are told what Abram's response was; but what a significant verse it is. He left the land of promise and went down to Egypt in search of food. From a human point of view it is eminently sensible, but from a spiritual point of view it is the first step to catastrophe. God had kept His promises for hundreds of miles. Granted, it was Abram who had been obedient, but it was God who had been faithful. Did Abram not think that God who had guided and provided for every step of the journey could do it now? In the crisis faith weakens. He leaves the land of promise and trust gives way to rationality. As he loses faith he loses the opportunity of discovering the answer which God could have given. He had walked by faith, but now he begins to walk by sight.

The Christian life is a delicate balance of hard headed rationality and apparently irrational obedience. God gave us minds to think things through, of course. But it is all too easy to use this as an excuse for not doing what deep inside we know we ought to do. God gave us minds, but we all know He has another way of speaking to us and challenging us. The world cannot understand it. When we are obedient to it rather than to our reason others think we are crazy. They wonder what has got into us. But we know. It is the imperative of God which we cannot deny and remain at peace. Throughout history those who have been obedient to it have been viewed by their contemporaries as at least a little strange and at worst rather mad. But often the next generation has seen them for what they were; men and women of faith. People who did the crazy thing for God, and it has called them saints.

But this is not Abram. When trouble threatens he denies God the opportunity of meeting his need. He leaves the land of promise. We may reason that it was the sensible thing to do, but the development of the story convinces us that he had not only stepped out of the land, he had stepped out of God's will.

No sooner is the decision taken than things begin to go wrong. This whole episode, thankfully brief, is a downward spiral in the life of a spiritual giant. As he reaches the borders of Egypt he is gripped by fear. There is little doubt that Pharaoh's reputation had gone before him. He was, after all, the most powerful person in the region. He could have exactly what he wanted, including whoever he wanted for his harem. Here is the problem. Sarai was exceptionally beautiful. To Abram there seemed little doubt that once Pharaoh saw her he would want her. But she was married to Abram. Pharaoh would do whatever it took to get her, including taking Abram's life. The fact that she was married would not deter him. Pharaoh could take her if she was a widow but not if she was Abram's wife. Abram realises that he is expendable.

Without any regard for his wife's feelings Abram hatches a cunning plot. If she is presented not as his wife but his sister it will solve all his problems, or so he thinks. Most importantly he will be able to save his own skin. But in addition he realises that if Pharaoh takes her, and if she makes a good impression, Abram himself will gain Pharaoh's favour. He will be able to bask in her glory and gain wealth because he is Sarai's brother.

With hindsight we can see that as soon as Abram deserted the way of faith things began to go from bad to worse. He was gripped with fear. Even then God did not feature in his thinking. His dependence on his own strength meant that he had to work it out for himself, and so we see a plan of intrigue and deceit is put into operation. The man of faith has become a cheat. It gets worse. Genesis 20:12 informs us that Sarai was, in fact, Abram's half sister. So his fabricated story was not a complete lie. It contained enough truth to enable Abram to justify it if he was questioned. But the point at issue is not how much truth there is in the story, but what Abraham's motives were. The person who had been driven by an overwhelming desire to do God's will is now consumed by self interest. Once he left the land of promise he was on a slippery slope. Deceit compounded selfishness.

How true to life this story is. So often we do what others recognize as being the rational and pragmatic thing, but deep inside we know that by doing it we are stepping out of the will of God. When things begin to go wrong we wonder why, but often we know. It is because we have moved out of the gracious providence of God and chosen to rely on our own ingenuity. But our ingenuity, like the rest of us is corrupt; and so we plan and work out our schemes. They do not make things better. In fact they compound the problem. To cap it all we retain enough regard for the truth to be able to justify our actions when we are challenged. We may fool everyone, except the God who continues to believe in us even when we cease to rely on Him.

What Abram anticipated did in fact happen. Sarai did appear attractive to Pharaoh. He did take her for his harem. Abram's life was saved and furthermore he gained Pharaoh's favour and considerable wealth because he was thought to be Sarai's brother. He must have thought everything had gone according to plan, just as he wanted. He got rich, but at the price of his own integrity. And then things began to go wrong. They always do! We do not have any details about the disease which Pharaoh and his household suffered and we must be careful not to read anything into scripture at this point. It does not say that they caught the disease from Sarai. But the consequence of Abram's sinful action was disease which manifested itself for all to see.

Nor do we know how Pharaoh concluded that Abram's plot was the cause, but he did. What a frightening moment it must have been for Abram when the truth had to come out. Pharaoh could easily have taken Abram's head as the price for his treachery. But the most amazing thing happens. Pharaoh lets him off. In fact he does more than that. He sends them all away and allows them to keep the goods they have gained by false pretences. In fact the personal ethics of Pharaoh the unbeliever put those of Abram to shame. We can only guess at the mood of Abram's heart as he left Egypt, but we know how we would have felt.

His return to the land of promise was about more than the route he took. Step by step he made his way back to the place where things had gone wrong so long ago. Physically it involved returning via the Negev. Spiritually it was about returning to the way of faith. The excursion into the human way of doing things had been a disaster. The journey to Egypt and his experiences there had left wounds on the soul, which needed to be healed and stains on the heart which needed to be cleansed. If only things could be as once they were, before he blew it. He needs forgiveness, cleansing and renewal. So, with a heavy heart he returns to the place where worship had been offered before, the place where things seemed to be clear, the place where sacrifice had been offered. There he sought God again.

The wonder is that the writer of Genesis includes this episode at all. If he had only been concerned to present Abram as a great man of faith he would have missed it out. But he has another purpose. It is to help the reader know that God chooses human beings, with all their weaknesses, as the people through whom his purposes are to be fulfilled. Even the best folk get it wrong sometimes. We may have been led by a gracious God into the place which he has promised for us, but we are all only one step away from the self-reliance which leads to deceit and disaster.

But Abram came back. The land of promise was his again. And we can come back too. The God who opened the way for Abram will open the way for us, and the God who received him back again will receive us too. He may have blown it, and he may blow it again, but God does not give up on His servants that easily.

The Parting of the ways
Genesis 13:5-18

It is clear that so far Lot had accompanied Abram, his uncle, on this epic journey (Genesis 12:4, 13:1). They travelled together but, as will become clear, Lot did not understand Abram's motives, nor did he share his vision. Lot was always there but he was not united with Abram in answering God's call or following God's leading. He just went along as did many others. As a member of the patriarchal family he had a share of the wealth they had acquired, and no doubt exercised some subordinate leadership role. Abram and Lot were in the same group but they were not of the same mind. They followed the same route, but they did not have the same heart. The story is a vivid illustration of what can happen when two leaders do not share the same vision, when they are driven by different motives. It has been repeated many times, not least in Christian circles, when division amongst the people results from division amongst the leadership.

Abram would have been a role model for Lot, his nephew. Lot was the observer. Abram was the mentor. Lot saw all that Abram did - every action and reaction, good and bad. Of course, he was present on the trip to Egypt and when Abram had got things wrong Lot had observed that too. It may be that whilst in Egypt Lot had picked up a taste for city life with all its bright lights and dark corners.

When relationships are not all they should be, when two people, especially leaders do not share the same vision it often takes one issue to bring things to a head. That's what happened here. Both Abram's and Lot's flocks and herds had increased in size. Pasture was scarce. It could not support them all. Something had to be done. Increased prosperity had sharpened the division between them and their herdsmen were quarrelling over which pasture their herds could graze. Let's not forget that from the point of view of the inhabitants of the land Abram's arrival represented a mass movement of economic migrants. It is not difficult to see that hostility from the Canaanites and Perizzites was a real possibility. It seemed the sensible thing to divide. Abram would go one way and Lot the other. The grazing would be shared and they stood less chance of antagonizing the natives of the land.

It is Abram who takes the initiative and his suggestion gives a deep insight into the way he regarded Lot. From Abram's point of view this was not falling out. It was simply expedient. How stupid to allow a situation of confrontation to develop when the whole land is before them. There is enough for them all, but not all together.

Graciously Abram gives Lot the choice. As leader of the group Abram could have chosen and sent Lot where he would, but instead he gives Lot first pick. Of course Lot chooses the best land. It is the Jordan plain, fertile, well-watered, great grazing. In fact it reminds him of how things were in Egypt. Could it be that the writer of Genesis wants us to understand that it was more than good grazing land which influenced Lot's choice? So off he goes with his tents, herds, herdsmen and families to occupy that portion of the land which he had chosen. There were cities there and Lot establishes camp near one of them, Sodom. Interestingly, before long he moved from living nearby to within the city (Gen 14:12).

So that leaves Abram with the rest, the less fertile land. What was he feeling like? He had been obedient to the call of God, left everything he knew and led a people on a trek of hundreds of miles in quest of a promised land. Despite his Egyptian diversion he was there; back on track with God and now standing in the place which God had promised him. No sooner was he there than the bubble bursts, the vision is smashed, and things begin to go wrong. Tensions break out in the family and there has to be a parting of the ways. Trying to do the right and gracious thing he offers Lot the choice, and finds that he is left with the worst land; the portion which Lot does not want. He tried to do the best and finished up with the worst. How would you have felt?

It is as Abram is reflecting on Lot's choice, and no doubt what he has been left with, that God speaks again. It is, in many ways, an echo of the earlier promise. But what significance it must have had for Abram in that moment. He knew as clearly as he could, that God would keep his word, but in that moment he needed the reassurance of God's promise again.

Sometimes we are all like that. We believe. We stake our whole lives on the promises of God. Like Abram we have no proof that it will work out. Like him we journey by faith. We just dare to believe God, even without the evidence. This is the faith by which we are justified. On the journey things work out well most of the time, at least we get by. But just occasionally things go badly. We try and do the right thing and finish up with a raw deal. It is at the emotional level that faith takes a battering. We believe, and will always believe, but in the dark moments we, like Abram, need God to speak again. It's not because we are weak. It is because we are human.

As they have reflected on the gospel story many have observed something similar in the life of Jesus. There are moments in His ministry where great choices have to be made and new resolve is required. It is then that God speaks, and even though the road leads to Calvary the Saviour receives the assurance he needs to enable him to see it through.

Faith can be strong, but emotionally we can take a battering. Those are the moments we need to hear God speak again. How important it is, therefore, at those very times, to put ourselves where God can speak more clearly and where we can hear more easily. The times when discipleship takes a battering are the very times when we ought to be found searching out the presence of God. When we can't understand what God is up to we ought to be allowing him to speak to us in worship, prayer, Bible study and the support of Christian friends. That is the worst time to place ourselves in a position which makes it even more difficult for God to get through.

To say that God's promise is simply an echo of the one made earlier is not the whole truth. In Abram's situation it is the new element which meant most. It was not just a reassuring word, but a confirmation of God's promise to give *all* the land to Abram and his offspring. He had, of course, just given half of it away, but that did not alter God's commitment. In ways which seemed a mystery to Abram the whole land would be his. God had promised, and somehow He would work it out.

As we have seen, Abram did not always get it right, but when he made mistakes he knew how to get back to where he ought to be. The mistakes need not lead to disaster. The mistakes may cast doubt on our commitment but they do not nullify God's commitment. We need to rediscover a confidence in the sovereignty of God. The dependability of God's promises is not weakened by our errors of judgment or lack of insight into how God will bring his promises to fulfilment.

With the promise comes another command. He is to go and walk through the land which God is giving to him. It was not enough to sit back and thank God for what He had promised. Abram had to go and embark on a pilgrimage of faith. With every step he was to believe that this land would be his one day. He was, by faith, to claim the ground as he walked. Once again faith needed to be expressed in action. So he moves off, travels the land, and eventually establishes a camp and builds an altar to the Lord. He has not got all the answers, but he is now able to live in the confidence of God's provision, and the strength of God's promises.

Caught up in conflict
Genesis 14:1-24

Of all the episodes in Abram's life, this is probably the most unfamiliar to many readers. The names make it difficult to read. The lack of background knowledge makes it difficult to understand. The message seems obscure. So we will have to work hard if we are to get to the heart of it. It will probably help to have a map available.

Part of the problem is that we are thinking about events which occurred so long ago that the exact location of some of the places mentioned in the story are now uncertain. Indeed, the fact that the writer gives alternative names, which appear in brackets in our translation, suggests that at the time of writing the names of some of the places mentioned had already changed. We are dealing with the political and military history during a 14 year period which was probably scarcely later than the middle of the second millennium BC. Of course, political and military history impinges on spiritual history and we must remember that the writer of Genesis is not primarily a political historian. Rather he wants us to understand how the Lord chose and guided Abram, and how He eventually fulfilled the promise which He had made. For the writer of Genesis our God is one who keeps his word. He is the Lord of earth and heaven who will not ultimately allow political unrest to frustrate His will.

It is clear that the rulers of the area which Abram had left, around Ur in Mesopotamia, had, ironically, sought to expand their domain into Canaan, the land which Abram had been promised and in which he was now living. The Kings of the city states in Canaan had been forced to pay tribute to the Mesopotamian kings, which they had done for 12 years. In the 13th year they rebelled against this unfair taxation, as it appeared to them; and it is this rebellion which prompted the invasion of Canaan. It is clear, however, that the Mesopotamian kings took the opportunity, whilst they were travelling to Canaan, to subdue other kingdoms on the way. What we have here is a glimpse into ancient imperial expansion.

So we have the four kings of Mesopotamia, headed by Kedorlaomer, facing the five rebellious kings of the Canaanite city states. In the battle which ensued the five city states were quickly defeated. In the panic which followed many were taken captive and their homes were plundered. Some tried to escape, but in the confusion fell into the tar pits which were common in that area. When the Kings of Sodom and Gomorrah deserted their battle lines others did the same and some escaped to the hills. We would probably never have heard of this event if it had not been for one of those who escaped. He brought sad news to Abram. Lot was amongst those who had been captured.

Interestingly, 'Abram' and 'Hebrew' is the kind of title which would never have been used by one Jew of another. This suggests, therefore, that this account came from an independent observer and some have even gone as far as to suggest that it was a rather derogatory term and ought to be understood as 'the migrant', 'the foreigner' or 'the alien'.

However, it is clear that, alien or not, Abram had won the confidence of his closest neighbours. He was in need and they all rallied to his aid. Together with the 318 trained men which Abram could muster they went in pursuit of the invading army in the hope that they may be able to secure Lot's release. With a relatively small army, but with a good strategy and the element of surprise they succeeded in throwing the enemy into confusion. Lot and his possessions are recaptured together with all the goods which the invading army had seized, other people they had captured and the women, whose fate in enemy hands must have been so severe that the writer mentions them particularly.

On his return Abram is greeted by two very different characters.

First there is the King of Sodom, a city already notorious for its wickedness. We need to remember that it was Abram who had led the army that conquered the invaders. He was the one who had secured the release of the captives and the recovery of possessions. The spoils of war were rightly his. Yet, with an attitude which says much about his moral character, the King of Sodom presents Abram with a proposition. He will take the people and Abram can keep the goods. But Abram had already made up his mind. He had not gone into battle to gain wealth or secure the spoils of war, but merely to gain the release of Lot his nephew. His integrity must remain intact. He has decided that he will not accept even a shoe lace through the favours of the King of Sodom. He will not give the King of Sodom the satisfaction of being able to say, at some future date, "I made Abram rich'. Implicitly Abram is committed to rely on the providence of God. He is part of a counter-culture which stands over against the sin and opulence of Sodom. Once again Abram demonstrates what it means to live by faith, trusting God and shunning what the world prizes.

In a complicated world like ours it is often difficult to know where the goods which we use come from or what the money we invest is used for. The fact that this is difficult does not absolve the Christian of responsibility. Like Abram so long ago we need to maintain our integrity. There can be no excuse for gaining wealth on the proceeds of sin, corruption and the exploitation of others. Like Abram, we too are committed to a counter culture in which a person's value is not determined by their wealth or possessions. We refuse to be tainted by the proceeds of sin. We trust that the God who provided all Abram's needs will provide ours too.

The other person who greeted Abram was Melchizedek. In view of the fact that he is mentioned several times elsewhere in the unfolding story of scripture we wish that more had been said about him. In a period when a person is identified by their genealogy Melchizedek is mentioned without one. His name means 'King of Righteousness' and he is described as a King and a priest. Indeed, without having any knowledge of his background he is identified as a priest of 'God Most High'. The writer wants us to understand that here we are dealing with a genuine believer and a priesthood which predates that Levitical priesthood which descended from Abram himself. Here is one who, though shrouded by mystery, represents a priesthood which did not depend of genealogy. This was straight from God Himself. This was the genuine article. Was the offering of bread and wine just for Abram's sustenance following the battle, or with the benefit of hindsight are we meant to grasp a deeper truth in the refreshment offered by this man who was at once both priest and king. There is no doubt that the subsequent writers of scripture recognized the profound significance of this event. Those who read it with the benefit of hindsight, especially Christians, have seen in this figure a 'type' of Christ. It is not difficult for us to understand how they make this connection. He is priest and king. He offers bread and wine. He is straight from God. He is King of Jerusalem. One wonders whether the crowds who lined Jesus' route into Jerusalem on Palm Sunday remembered this story and wondered at the presence of a 'new' Melchizedek in their midst.

As one who had conquered kings, Abram was now literally, king of kings. Yet no matter how powerful he may be in the eyes of the world he is still a servant of God, one who follows God's pathway even though sometimes it may be a tortuous route. Melchizedek's visit and the blessing which he gives to Abram re-established

Abram's correct position in the reader's mind. If the account of Abram's victory had created an unfortunate impression of greatness, Melchizedek restores the correct order of priorities. . And for Abram Melchizedek's blessing brings the reassurance of God's continuing providential care. The victory and deliverance had not been because of Abram, but of God. Abram knew the blessing of this great God once again. There is no doubt that it was in humility and gratitude that Abram offered his tithe.

Establishing the covenant
Genesis 15

From what is probably one of the most unfamiliar passages in Abram's story we move to one of supreme importance. In the unfolding story of scripture it is a landmark.

The stress, tension and physical exertion which Abram had endured in the mission to release Lot from captivity, brought all sorts of fears to the surface in Abram's mind. In the military campaign that he had just undertaken he had won a victory and accomplished his purposes, but he had also incurred the wrath of a very powerful military alliance. After all, they were trying to dominate the whole region. They would probably seek retaliation. If that happened where would Abram turn for help? How would he cope?

When the victory had been won and the spoils of war had been gained Abram had refused to compromise with sin. He had not kept even a shoe lace of the plunder which was rightly his. Even when it was his right he would not compromise his integrity. His actions were admirable, but were they prudent? He had denied himself material gain for the sake of his integrity, but when all was said and done he was still left with the worst grazing land, and a great number of mouths to feed. Who would provide for their future security?

It is to such a fearful heart that God speaks - 'the word of the Lord came to Abram…' (v1). For all those who know the Bible that is a very familiar phrase. We come across it again and again in the prophets. It is repeated here in verse 4, but it is never found elsewhere in the Pentateuch. Clearly, we are heading for a significant, if not unique event. Nor was it to last but a moment. A close examination of the text reveals that it began one night ('Look up at the heavens and count the stars…' v5) continues all the following day and through the following night (v12,17). Here we have an encounter with God of some duration and of singular importance.

Once again God takes the initiative. When Abram is feeling fearful and wretched God seeks him out. The Almighty seeks to still Abram's fearful heart. God affirms that He Himself is Abram's shield and great reward. Although Abram cannot see God's shield protecting him, he can count on God's presence and rely on His protection. Life has been difficult and challenging. Where is Abram's reward for doing what he has done? It can be very difficult to keep doing the right thing if you never have anything to show for it and no one appreciates what you are doing. But God who is Abram's protector is also Abram's great reward. The reward is God Himself.

We all know that when we feel as Abram did a word of assurance is important, but that alone is often incapable of stilling restless hearts. Abram wanted a bit more detail. Promises are great, but we all want more than that sometimes, especially when all the evidence seems to suggest that the promises are just empty words. With a human frailty with which we can all identify Abram lays the questions before God. It's alright God making promises, but Abram is still childless. In fact as things stand Eliezer, his adopted son is the only heir he has.

We have no details about Eliezer, except that he came from Damascus. We know that Abram had passed through Damascus and it was maybe at this time that Eziezer's parents joined Abram's household. We also know from ancient texts that adoption was practised in the ancient world and that the adopted child inherited the possessions of the parents if they died without any heirs born to them. If, however, a child was born to them that child would become the heir rather than the adopted child.

Once again God speaks a word of promise. This person, Eliezer, would not be the heir. Abram would have a son of his own. Through this personal struggle Abram was learning what so many find very difficult, that God's delays ought not to be understood as God's denials. Abram had trusted God's promises, but it had become increasingly difficult to do so, especially when there was so little evidence to support the promise. The stress of recent events had brought to the surface the fear that the promise would never be fulfilled. After all, Abram had staked everything on this. How could he be sure?

Like most of us Abram needed to see things differently. He needed a new perspective. God tries to help him, "Count the stars..." (v5). Of course he could not, and neither can we with the most powerful telescope available to us. But God knows how many there are. He knows everything. What we call mysteries are not mysteries to Him. If we could, for a moment, catch a glimpse of things from God's perspective faith might not seem so great a challenge. It is only so challenging to us because we don't have all the answers and can't see the total picture. Faith involves trusting for the part we cannot see based on the evidence revealed in the part we can see.

Interestingly, the quotation of the Divine voice in v5 is interrupted by the writer's comment indicating that the stars bring two lessons. The first concerns acknowledging that we are ignorant about some things which are crystal clear to God; and the second concerns the numerical growth of Abram's descendents. Abram would just settle for one son, but God promises as many descendents as the stars. To Abram it seemed impossible. But it was not impossible to God, and from our perspective we can only marvel at the wonderful fulfilment of God's promise. Of course, when we consider Abram's descendents we need to remember that we are not just thinking about those whose physical ancestry can be traced to him, but all those who are his children by faith (see Rom 4:6-17).

The illustration of the stars must have been enough to convince Abram, for Abram believed the Lord, and here we have this phrase again, it was "credited to him as righteousness". Our study of Abram's character so far in the story had revealed someone who is short of perfect. He makes mistakes. Sometimes his motives are not all they ought to be. In short, he does not have the righteousness which God requires and which God's nature demands. But here again we stumble on the one single truth which lies at the heart of the Christian gospel. Faith is credited to him as righteousness. He is counted righteous even when he is not, or not righteous enough, because he has faith. To simply take God at his word, to believe Him, when there is no evidence that His promise will ultimately be fulfilled is the faith for which Abram is famed through the rest of scripture. He had not received the fulfilment of God's promise, nor could he do anything to bring it about. He was absolutely helpless. All he could do was to look to the greatness and faithfulness of God. The fulfilment of the promise was God's responsibility not Abram's. It was this simple, yet challenging, reliance on God's promise which enabled a relationship with God, even when the righteousness which God requires was lacking. Or to put it another way, faith was the fitting response on Abram's part to the initiative of grace which God had already taken in choosing him.

God's promise concerned not only a son, but also a land which his descendants would inhabit. God reiterates the promise now. Once again we have a hint at the foundation of Abram's faith. He may have little evidence on which to base his faith, but he has the personal experience of God's guidance already given. The God who repeats his former promise is the One who had already proved his faithfulness to Abram. So far God had kept His word. He had remained faithful. There is enough evidence here to enable Abram to trust God to fulfil His promise in its entirety, as He had fulfilled it partially already.

Abram's response is absolutely understandable and absolutely natural. The evidence of God's faithfulness already given seems insufficient. So he asks, as we do so often, "How can I know...?" (v8). It is this desire for more concrete evidence that leads to one of the most solemn moments in Old Testament history, for God is about to establish a covenant with Abram. It would go down in history as a foundation stone on which all Jewish and subsequent Christian faith would be built.

Of course, this is not the first time God has entered into a covenant with his people (see Gen 8:21-22) but it is arguably the most significant. To reassure Abram that God's promise was entirely reliable God enters into a solemn treaty, something which would be well known as a binding agreement between two parties, a social and political convention of the Near East.

Abram is to bring five sacrifices. We do not know why these particular animals and birds were chosen, but we are told what is to be done with them. They are to be cut in half and two piles of the carcasses are to be made. It is interesting to remember at this point that the Hebrew technical term is to 'cut a covenant'. Inevitably it involves the shedding of blood and the loss of life. For greater detail we need to turn to other passages of scripture. - Jeremiah 34:8-19 is helpful. The solemn agreement was made by passing between the two halves of the carcasses. The covenant is ratified by the blood of the animals which had been slaughtered. The implication of passing between them is that the people who do so agree that if their part of the covenant is broken they ought to be made like the animals. One's life was the cost of breaking the covenant. In this dramatic way God was telling Abram that he could "know for certain" (v13).

Abram does not receive a direct answer to his question, "How can I know?" Instead he is given a glimpse into God's timescale, an outline of the events which must take place before his descendents inherit the land (v12-16). His is not the time to occupy the land. He did not have the military might to overcome those who lived there, nor could he adequately occupy it. From another point of view it was not yet the time for God's judgment to fall on the Amorites, for their sin had not reached its full measure - it was not yet completed.

Here we encounter the God of history who, for a brief moment, draws back the curtain to enable Abram to see His greater purposes. He knows the moral state of each nation. His people will be subject to bondage but the liberation from slavery and subsequent possession of the promised land would be the time when God's judgment would fall on the inhabitants of the land. The Lord governs the nations, knows the heart and responds in judgment or blessing through the events which, by secular observers, are described as international affairs.

It is not uncommon, in scripture, for fire or flames to indicate the presence of God Himself, and here we encounter just such a manifestation. As, when a covenant was cut between two people, they would pass between the halves of the sacrifice; so here God himself, in the flames of a smoking brazier and a torch, passes between them. Of course, if the covenant had been between two people they would have both passed between, but here there is no call for Abram to do so. He is simply the observer. It is God, who by solemn covenant, makes the commitment. This is all of grace.

The Lord cut a covenant with Abram that day using the most solemn form of oath. Even God could not be more serious about this than He is. In principle the land was Abram's already. It was as certain as God's word, for such is the sovereignty of God's promise. The land may currently be occupied by other peoples, but it was the land of promise and nothing can be more certain than the promises of God.

Tension in the home
Genesis 16

Through the story recounted in chapter 15 Abram had learned a lesson which we all must learn: God's delays are not God's denials. The fact that God's promises are not fulfilled straight away does not mean that they will not be fulfilled at all. In theory, of course, that is a significant lesson; but the experiences of the human heart do not always sit easily with the theory. We believe, but we want to see just a little bit of evidence that our belief is not misplaced and that God will keep his word. When, over a long period of time, that does not happen we begin to feel that either God has left us or that he needs a hand.

Abram had been living in Canaan for ten years. He was getting older, and so was Sarai his wife. If the chances of Abram having a child had been remote when first the promise was made, they seemed to be getting more remote with every passing year. Furthermore, every time God renewed his promise to Abram it compounded Sarai's sense of failure. The very situation which called for persistent faith in Abram made Sarai feel more and more inadequate.

In the ancient world there were culturally acceptable methods of addressing the problem of childlessness. Adoption was one option, and we have already seen that Abram had adopted a son, but that God had confirmed that he, Eliezer, would not be the one through whom the promise would be fulfilled. In doing so God had told Abram that "a son coming from your own body will be your heir". There is no mention of Sarai here. It is not surprising, therefore, that after ten years she begins to wonder whether the son which would be Abram's would also be hers. Was there another way?

In Abram's culture there was just such a way. If the wife who was unable to have children had a slave girl she could give the slave to her husband to become a surrogate mother. We need to remind ourselves at this point that everything a slave possessed was the possession of the slave's master or mistress. That included children. So, in this situation the slave would bear the child, but the wife (the slave's mistress) would have jurisdiction over the child. Ancient texts confirm that this practice was sometimes undertaken and that subsequently the child would be legally adopted in order to maintain the right of inheritance. The Bible is not endorsing this practice, but merely reminding us that in that cultural situation it was an option.

It is not surprising, therefore, that after ten years wait Sarai thinks that this is the way ahead and makes the suggestion to Abram. She is not convinced that this is God's plan, but 'perhaps' it is (v2). The fact that this is so readily accepted as a possible solution by Abram reminds us how difficult this great man of faith found it to go on believing when he did not have any evidence. Once again, as in the Egyptian episode, faith was beginning to step aside and reason was moving in. So Abram agrees, "Yes dear!" It may be that Hagar joined Abram and Sarai during the Egyptian trip. In any event she was the maidservant of Sarai and required to obey Sarai's commands.

The deed is done and Hagar conceives. On paper, at least, all is going according to plan. But Sarai had not expected the emotional upheaval which this caused. The pregnancy had elevated Hagar's status within the home. She had got one up on her mistress. She had done what Sarai was unable to do and the baby she was carrying gave her an importance which she had never had before. No doubt Sarai had expected that things would go very smoothly and that even though Hagar was carrying a child her relationship with Sarai would continue just as before, but the new attitude of Hagar was unbearable. Believing that she has just grounds for complaint she goes to Abram and expects him to put Hagar in her place. What she wants is understanding and support from her husband in a situation which she finds intolerable.

That is not what she gets. On the contrary, Abram reminds her that all this has come about because of her suggestion. It had been her idea and she just had to learn to cope with it. No help there. The last thing Abram wanted was to be placed in a position of having to decide between Sarai to whom he was married and Hagar who was carrying his child. He avoids the difficult issue by reminding Sarai that Hagar is *her* maidservant. She must do what she thinks best. It was not up to him to address such an issue.

One can only imagine the tension which this produced between Abram and Sarai. Life in the home at this time must have been very difficult. There is a breakdown in the relationship between Abram and Sarai, and between Sarai and Hagar. It was not a good place to be. But when all was said and done Sarai was the mistress and Hagar was the slave, and everything about Sarai's attitude emphasized that relationship. Hagar was swiftly removed from the elevated status which she believed her pregnancy had brought, and now it was her life which was made unbearable, to the extent that Hagar was even ill-treated. She could take it no longer and eventually does what every slave dreams of, she runs away.

The extent of the punishment which could be inflicted on runaway slaves gives a clear indication of the desperation which Hagar felt. Where was she to go? She did what many others have done in similar situations; she makes her way back home. From the misery in which she was living the only place which she thought she could feel comfortable and loved was back in Egypt. So she takes the road to Shur, the eastern district of Egypt.

Travel in such circumstances would have been perilous. She was pregnant and had to cross the desert. Her life depended on being able to reach the next oasis, spring or well. In fact, it was maybe the existence of the spring which had determined the course of the road. It was at one such spring that the messenger of God found her. She was not one of the chosen race; in everyone's opinion she was a nobody, and in her state of mind she agreed with them. But God sought her out. In the first book of the Bible we are discovering what Peter so much later found it so difficult to accept; that God shows no partiality (Acts 10:34).

The reason for the messenger's question, of course, is not that the messenger does not know Hagar's circumstances, but that it is important for Hagar to open up those circumstances and her wretched life to the God who had sought her out. Yet the God who had come to comfort and rescue did not avoid the costly challenge which was necessary for things to be put right. She should go back to her mistress and submit to her. Humble pie was placed firmly on her menu. She had been used and abused, but to run away was not the answer. Yet the God who requires the difficult but right thing is also the God who speaks deep into her situation and need with a word of promise.

Maybe she, as a member of Abram's household, had heard the oft repeated promise which God had made to him. Now there was a similar one for her. Like Abram's descendents, hers too will be too numerous to count.

There follows a little poem and for us to grasp its full meaning we need to consult the footnotes in our Bibles. Hagar had thought that no one had heard her tears as she fled from a household where her life had become a misery. But God had heard and she is to call the child which she is carrying Ishmael, which means 'God hears'. To our western minds donkeys are a symbol for stupidity, but not to the writers of scripture. A quick glance at other verses (e.g. Job 39:5-8, Hosea 8:9) reveals them as symbols of freedom and independence. Once we realize that, the rest of the little poem seems to make far more sense. It is the fierce independence of Hagar's descendents which will set them over against their neighbours. In fact, through this short verse God is preparing Hagar for the separation which will come between her and Ishmael her child and Abram's household.

Who is this mysterious messenger whom she encountered on the way? Initially described as an angel, now his true identity is revealed. It is God himself who has sought her out. In that moment of realization the deflated, frightened and miserable Hagar grasps the great truth which was to be revealed to the whole world in Jesus. God had not just sent his messenger in search of her, though that would have been wonderful enough. He had come himself. In all her lostness, feeling that no one knew her pain, God had seen her. And even more amazing, she had seen the one who had seen her. She, the slave from an alien race, had seen God and lived to tell the tale. So amazing was the event that it demanded a lasting memorial. The well was all she had, so she renames it. Beer Lahai Roi is to be its name from this moment on.

In the language of Genesis there is a pun here which is lost in English. A glance at the footnotes will help us to tease it out. Beer Lahai Roi means 'the well of the living one who sees me'. In a desert place where one lived so close to death, God had shown Himself to be the living One and He had seen her when she thought no one knew her pain.

Despite the earlier intentions of Sarai, Ishmael was not adopted as her own son. As our thoughts move from this painful episode to the next great chapter in this unfolding story we may be tempted to forget Hagar and Ishmael. Their life in the household of Abram, and Sarai, cannot have been easy. Her return home had been costly and her presence was no doubt a continuing source of pain to Sarai, but the God who had sought her out in her darkest moment had a plan and purpose for her and her son too. It would be different from the plan He had for Abram, but in a few chapters we are to be reminded that the God of the Jew had a purpose for the descendents of Ishmael too.

Known by name and sign
Genesis 17

Thirteen years had elapsed between the close of chapter 16 and the opening of chapter 17. It must have been very difficult for Abram to go on believing that God would keep His word and grant him a son and heir. With every passing year the fulfilment of the promise seemed more and more unlikely, at least from a human point of view. It is the writer to the Letter to the Hebrews who reminds us that by this time Abram was "as good as dead" (Heb 11:12). But as this chapter opens we are confronted with a God who speaks to Abram again, announcing Himself as God Almighty, El-Shaddai. The human limitations on Abram's situation are obvious, but they are no obstacle to an Almighty God.

We need to remember that when God made the covenant with Abram in Genesis 15 it was unlike any human covenant. Human covenants were agreements struck between two parties and each one had a part to play. They signified their agreement by each walking between the sacrificed carcasses. But in this case it was only God, as a flaming brazier and torch who walked between them. This was not a bargain struck between equals. It was a relationship in which God was the initiator. He pledged Himself to Abram. It was all of grace.

Now God comes to confirm that covenant and to renew the promise made so many years earlier. As He does so we stumble on a truth often ignored. Even though the relationship with God is founded entirely on God's grace it is not without obligations. Indeed, it is precisely because it is all of grace that the obligations are demanding. Relationship lies at the heart of covenant. Within a relationship we cannot legislate for every eventuality. Circumstances are constantly changing. Yet within a relationship we seek to live in a way which is pleasing and not hurtful to the other. This lies at the heart of God's requirements stated here. Abram is to walk before God and be blameless.

Walking is about movement, progress. Think of the other occasions when Biblical characters walked with God (see Gen 3:8, 5:24, 6:9 for examples). It is about circumstances constantly changing yet the relationship being maintained despite all the things which may challenge it. To put it in more theological language; holiness must be dynamic and not static if it is to be Biblical holiness. Holiness is about the nature of the journey and not the destination at which we hope, one day, to arrive. Essentially holiness is the nature of our relationship with God.

Abram is to walk *before* God. We must not think of this as though God were following! This is not the 'before' of the procession, but the 'before' of the audience, as one would appear before a monarch. It is about living in the presence of God, and living in such a way that our conduct does not intentionally offend the God who accompanies us on the journey. Abram is required to be blameless. Sometimes he will make mistakes, as we have seen so far in our studies. Faith can falter even in the best people. But his intention must be right. He is not free to live within this covenant relationship and ignore the demands it makes. The grace of God requires nothing less than a whole-hearted desire to live in a way which is pleasing to God.

The word of God Almighty to Abram so long ago is, in a profound sense, a word to all who would be in a relationship with God. The relationship is founded on the grace of God alone, but the relationship involves living for the other, in this case God Himself. It is dynamic not static, growing with changing circumstances. It is about living every moment in the divine presence and seeking, as best we can, so to live that our whole lives may be a worthy offering to God. We are not in a relationship with God because of our conduct, as though we had to gain that relationship by being good. But a distinctive lifestyle grows naturally from the nature of the God to whom we are bound in covenantal relationship. To be holy is to be different. Different from the rest, because of the relationship we have with God, different because we are bound to him by covenantal love.

How does Abram respond to a God who pledges Himself in sovereign grace? He falls on his face in worship before the majesty of God Almighty. There is no arguing here. No questioning as there had been before. Worship and surrender were the only fitting responses. It was just Abram and God now. Everything else would be an intrusion. In that moment nothing else mattered.

To an old man, with faltering faith and a track record which was less than perfect God Almighty confirms a covenant and renews a promise. But this time there is more detail. Abram had already been promised that many would own him as their father, but now it is amplified. He is to be the father of many nations. Kings will descend from his line. All Abram's descendents would inherit this covenantal relationship and God would give the whole land of Canaan to them. This covenant is to be everlasting. God is committed to Abram and his people, and they are to be committed to Him.

So profound is this relationship that it demands two things. They both indicate that even though Abram has travelled a long way in answer to the call of God and in hope of the promise being fulfilled, from this point the journey is to be different. They put a marker down. There is no going back now. What was a private relationship between Abram and God moves into a public arena. Their relationship can be a private matter no longer.

The first sign of this new and deeper relationship is that Abram is to have a new name. Of course, names in the ancient world almost invariably had a significant meaning for the person bearing them. Abram, meaning 'exalted father' had been his name up to this point. Now emphasizing the amazing bounty of God's promise he is to be called Abraham meaning 'father of many'. He had difficulty understanding how he could have even one child. But God was promising many! One wonders how this would be understood by his contemporaries. Rather difficult to bear when you are ninety-nine years old without a child and with a wife known to be barren! Even Abraham's name was to point to the God Almighty who was able to do what no one could imagine. As you read verses 3-8 notice how often God speaks of what he is going to do. *I will make...I will establish.... I will give.....* This is all about the amazing power of God working in and through one whom He has chosen in grace. And it is all made possible not because Abram was good enough, but because he dared to believe that God would keep His promises.

Commitment, of course, is a two-way process. God had committed Himself unconditionally to Abraham, but now Abraham had to commit himself and his heirs unconditionally to God. Such commitment required a sign and circumcision was the one God chose. It would be a constant reminder to each successive generation that they were included within this gracious covenantal relationship. It was not optional but obligatory. To refuse the sign was to break the covenant and forfeit the promised inheritance (v14). Mercifully, women were not required to undergo any such surgery, as they have been in some cultures, but this does not mean that they are beyond the covenant. They were an integral part of the family and as such, included, as were slaves, members of other races and all social classes who were part of the covenantal community.

Often this raises searching questions in those who seek a closer understanding of scripture. Why was this sign chosen? What makes circumcision so special? We need to acknowledge that we will never be able to gain a complete answer to all our questions on this, or so many other issues. They are buried too deep in the reasoning of almighty love. Maybe, by acknowledging this, we are inadvertently stumbling on a profound truth. Like the nature of the covenant it is simply beyond human reasoning. It becomes a matter, not of working out why it should be so, but of simply obeying because God requires it. That is the heart of the covenant relationship. Abraham's journey so far has convinced us that too often we get into difficulties when we exchange the way of faith for the way of reason. Maybe this is another powerful reminder that to obey when we cannot work out why is part of what it means to be included in this covenant.

There is another significant element which we must not miss. We see this truth clearest when we compare what is required here with what was practised in other contemporary cultures. When we examine ancient history we discover that circumcision was being practised; but almost invariably at puberty. It marked the transition from childhood to manhood. There are later Biblical references to this e.g. Gen 34:24. It is the requirement to practise circumcision on infants which is distinctively different here. The essence of this must, therefore, be that this is a sign of a relationship with God offered to them before they are able to do anything to earn, much less deserve, it. In essence the rite emphasizes the grace of God. They are included, not because of what they are but because of what God is. Not because of what they have done, but because of what God has done.

In a profound sense this encounter with God marks a new beginning for Abraham. That is why he is to have a new name. No longer is the covenant simply personal and in a sense private. It is now inclusive and accompanied by a ritual which will bring a constant reminder that he and his descendants are to be a covenant people. It marked a new beginning for Sarai too, and so she also is given a new name. She had discovered the hard way that no surrogate mother would do. Abraham is to be the father, but she is to be the mother. The new name is a symbol for a new status and a new kind of relationship, for the covenant is for her too.

It all seemed too remarkable to be true. Who ever heard of a man having a son when he was a hundred, and that when his wife was ninety! Even in worship before the Almighty God who would make it happen Abraham laughs as he thinks about it. Indeed, whenever Abraham saw or spoke to the son which would be born to him he would be reminded of the moment when he laughed in astonishment at the promise of God; for his son would be called Isaac, which means 'he laughs'!

But what about Ishmael? Was there a share of blessing for him too? In reply God allays all Abraham's fears. Despite his faltering faith God would fulfil His promise. He had a purpose for Ishmael too. Ishmael would not be excluded from blessing as Abraham feared. He is to have descendents too. Twelve will be rulers and he is to be the father of a nation as well. Despite all Abraham's misgivings God speaks a word of assurance. The Lord had it in hand all the time. Yet despite the fact that Ishmael is to know God's blessing, the particular blessings of the covenant relationship with its promise of land and blessings which would overflow to others are reserved for Isaac and his descendents.

Once the requirements of the covenant were known all that was required was for them to be fulfilled. This was no time to delay. So, on that very day, Abraham circumcised himself, Ishmael, and every male in his household and all those in Ishmael's household. Whatever their status or nationality, they were part of the covenant people by virtue of their relationship to Abraham. From that moment it would be performed on every male at the age of eight days, bearing witness to the fact that God's grace, not human merit was the foundation on which this covenant was built, and that this grace enfolded all.

As the story unfolds we see that the covenant made with God and witnessed through circumcision bound the nation to God and to one another. The covenant itself was based on God's sovereign choice and His amazing grace. Even though later there were those who lost sight of it and placed the emphasis on the human merit of keeping the law, the principle did not change, only the human perception of it. It is in Romans 4 that Paul reminds his readers of this principle again, and he echoes it again and again. We are placed in a right relationship with God not because of our merit but because of God's grace, and faith is the only fitting response. Abraham learned that, sometimes the hard way. It is the foundation of every true relationship with God. God has promised it! I believe it! That settles it!

Three visitors
Genesis 18:1-15

Sometimes in Shakespeare's plays one of the characters steps out of their role in the play and, for a brief moment, addresses the audience. It is a literary device which the playwright uses to make sure that the audience keeps up with the plot. We get the same kind of thing in the passage which we are now considering. The writer of Genesis wants the reader to know the identity of the visitors, but as the story begins it appears that Abraham does not realize who they are. It was 'the Lord' who appeared to Abraham, but when he looked up he saw 'three men'.

Notwithstanding that, Abraham offers the visitors a warm welcome and a level of hospitality which is surprising, even for the society in which he lived. He runs to them, despite the heat of the day. Could it be that he suspects that there is more to them than meets the eye? Does one bow so low for every visitor? It all seems to be on the spur of the moment, yet he clearly feels a great sense of honour if they would accept his invitation. Nor does the translation help us; 'my Lord' (v3) is equally well translated 'O Lord'. It's all very intriguing. Even though, in his society, one would be expected to offer hospitality to passing strangers Abraham's attitude to these three mysterious visitors leaves the reader feeling that he suspected they were more than they appeared to be.

Here we have another example of the way in which God encounters people, especially in Old Testament narrative. He makes Himself known through manifestations which, at first appear to be ordinary but which, for those who can discern the true meaning, are anything but. We have already seen how, in chapter 15, God manifests His presence through a smoking brazier and a blazing torch. Here again God is coming to encounter Abraham. We know that, because the writer has let us in on the secret as the chapter begins, but Abraham is not sure. In one respect they are just visitors, but Abraham's behaviour indicates that even as this episode begins he suspects that there is more to them than that.

This raises all sorts of questions for us. Why does God manifest himself in this way? It seems as though he deliberately tries to encounter people through the ordinary, which they subsequently realize is extraordinary. Rather than making His presence obvious from the beginning He wants people to work it out for themselves. Does Abraham's ultimate recognition depend on his own spiritual insight? Could it be that when God manifests Himself, those who have a living faith are able to discern His presence whilst others never make that recognition at all. Here we have stumbled on a powerful insight into the way God encounters people today. Maybe we would encounter Him more often if we had the faith which is able to discern His presence. Maybe Abraham's behaviour towards these visitors indicates that, whilst he was initially unsure of their true identity, he offered the level of hospitality which should be given if it were a divine visitation. It might be God himself coming to call!

In any event, they accept his invitation and, as would be the case in many of our homes, panic sets in. Sarah needs to get baking and the servant needs to get butchering. It is as they are eating that we are given a clue to the real reason for their visit. Abraham has travelled many miles and repeatedly God has promised that he would be the father of many. Abraham, failing to see how this could possibly happen has tried to help God out. Was adoption the way? No. Was it to be surrogate motherhood? No. In every case the promise has been confirmed. The covenant has been established through sacrifice and confirmed through circumcision. Yet so far Abraham has been the one to receive the promise and the confirmation. But Sarah was to play a crucial role in this too. She was to be the mother of Abraham's son in fulfilment of God's promise.

Now these visitors arrive and we begin to discover that the confirmation which they brought was not just for Abraham, but for Sarah too. As they are eating Sarah is within the tent. It's easy to hear conversations through a tent wall, as anyone who has been camping knows! As the visitors talk with Abraham outside the tent Sarah overhears. The promise is that within the next twelve months she is to become pregnant. At her age it is unbelievable, even laughable! So she laughs as she considers the possibility. What she does not realize is that not only could she hear them, they could hear her. So the visitors ask why she laughed. More significantly, they are clearly able to read her thoughts. She had thought it an impossibility (v12). They thought she said it (v13).

To laugh at a sensible statement made by honoured guests is an insult. It had just been a spontaneous response to an unbelievable statement. But now she knows that they had heard her. The human reaction is obvious. 'I did not laugh', she said. 'Oh yes you did' was the reply. Everyone knew the truth. One can imagine the conversation which ensued between Abraham and his wife after the visitors had left; his repeated accusation and her repeated denial. It's all very human.

The important thing is that Sarah had heard the promise for herself. There was to be no more speculation about adoption or surrogate motherhood. The baby would come from her. The very assertion may seem so remarkable to her that it makes her chuckle, but that is no obstacle to God. Nothing is too hard for him (v14). Now she knew. She had heard it too, through a tent wall. Her days of barrenness were over. She would be the mother of a nation.

As we look back on this brief episode it seems as though the prime purpose of the visit was to bring this reassurance to Sarah. Despite all her misgivings God was a match for the situation. He had determined and nothing was to stand in the way of His will being fulfilled. If Sarah was to become the channel through which God's purposes were to be fulfilled instead of an obstacle to their fulfilment she needed to hear the promise for herself. But she needed to hear it in a way that enabled her to accept it. She was a different personality to Abraham. He could take a direct word from the Lord, even though he doubted that it would be fulfilled. She needed to hear it by overhearing it!

There are people like that today. We must not feel that just because we do not hear direct words from the Lord He is not speaking to us. Some of us envy those who seem to be so clear about guidance, when we struggle to know the way ahead. But just because we find that God seems to be speaking to others more than He is speaking to us it does not mean that we are forgotten. God had a plan for Abraham, but He had a plan for Sarah too. He found a way of communicating that plan to them both; but the way was different for each of them. It was a way which was appropriate for their personality. Sometimes guidance comes with a deep, profound inner conviction which we cannot deny. But for many of us those times are rare. More often it is like a nudge from the Lord. We may not even recognize that it is from Him at all. But He is in control. He is shaping the path of our journey to bring us into His perfect will. The voice of God may sometimes shout at us, and sometimes it will be like overhearing a conversation through the wall of a tent. But it will still be His voice. Just because God does not speak to others as He speaks to us it does not mean that He does not speak to them at all. How much distrust and suspicion would be removed from Christian fellowship if we could just grasp this truth. God finds His own way of getting through to us. We ought not to be surprised if that is different for each one, because we are all different personalities. The variety of ways which God uses to speak His word into our lives is a measure of His grace.

Yet even though there is a variety in the methods of communication there is a consistency in the message which is delivered. The truth was told to both Abraham and Sarah in different ways, but it was the same truth. We need to remember that in a generation which sees everything as relative, where absolutes are seen as an indicator of intolerance and prejudice. In our fellowship and in our evangelism we need to recognize the variety of methods which God uses to communicate His truth. But the truth of the gospel, once for all delivered to the saints, is non-negotiable.

The Prayer that tries to understand
Genesis 18:16-33

The visitors had accomplished their mission. Sarah as well as Abraham had heard God's promise again. The details were clearer now, even though they were still difficult to understand and accept. But as far as the visitors were concerned, their job was done. They should be on their way.

We can imagine Abraham accompanying them along the road as they leave in the direction of Sodom. It was the home of Lot and his family, but its wickedness was already proverbial and it's not difficult to see how their attention was fixed upon it. Maybe Abraham was wondering how a righteous God would react. Would He allow the sin of Sodom to go unpunished for ever? What would that say about His justice and integrity?

We would do well to remember that Abraham had met the rulers and people of Sodom during his expedition to rescue Lot. So we can understand the mixed emotions which must have been in his heart. He acknowledges the sin of the people, but he feels for them because he knows them. Many of us can identify with these emotions as we seek to live under the standards of the Kingdom in a world which does not acknowledge the Lord to whom we belong.

Whether the justice issue was in Abraham's mind we do not know, but we are told that it was in the Lord's. He had called Abraham to a special role as leader of his own people. He is to direct his children to keep the way of the Lord by doing what is right and just. But God is the source of righteousness and justice. The obligation to lead others gives to Abraham the privileged insight of being able to know the Lord's intentions. The righteousness of God cannot allow sin and evil to go unpunished. God's integrity is at stake and Abraham must understand that very clearly if he is to lead God's people effectively.

Christian leadership can sometimes be very costly, not least because the clearer we understand the mind of God the clearer we are about his dealings with people. From a human point of view it is easier to keep quiet and mislead people into believing that God is so loving that sin and injustice can be tolerated. But the integrity of God is at stake. Once we have understood that God is righteous, just and loving we have new responsibilities. To understand the mind of God places an awesome burden upon us, but it is the price of godly leadership.

Yet God's integrity demands that he does not act on hearsay evidence. He needs to discover for himself whether what has been reported to Him is true. He will not condemn without first discovering the truth. How much pain would be avoided in human relationships if we all behaved in this way? How much pain has been caused through hasty judgments being pronounced on the strength of hearsay evidence which later proved false? That is not God's way, and it ought not to be ours.

It is difficult to understand exactly what happened at this point in the story. We are told that the men turned away and went towards Sodom but Abraham remained standing before the Lord (v22). The NIV footnote informs us that some ancient texts have it the other way round "the Lord remained standing before Abraham". Is the Lord one of the messengers? In which case two move off towards Sodom, or is the Lord present in addition to the three messengers? We cannot know for certain, and clearly this is anthropomorphic language. What matters, however, is that Abraham is given the privilege of a private conversation with the Lord.

The quality of Abraham's relationship with God was such that he felt able to share his concerns and questions. We find the same thing again and again in scripture, especially in the Psalms. To question what God does, to try and understand His mind when His actions seem to challenge what we believe about Him, are signs not of spiritual weakness but of a deep relationship with God. It's OK to feel angry with God and tell Him! And it's OK to question His proposed actions when they seem unjust, as Abraham does.

There are several ways in which the conversation between Abraham and the Lord has been understood. Some see it as Abraham striking a bargain with God; as though God had intended to destroy Sodom, but then Abraham haggles with God as one would do when buying a second-hand car. He's trying to get a more acceptable deal. Such an interpretation is deeply flawed, not least because it betrays a fundamental misunderstanding about prayer. Those who interpret this passage in that way see prayer as a means of getting God to do, or not to do as the case may be, what we want. That can't be right. God is not reluctant to bestow His blessings. He does not have to be worn down so that we can get the best deal. Jesus, when speaking about prayer reminds us that God is our loving Father. He does not have to be worn down, as the knocking on the door might wear down a reluctant neighbour. The emphasis of Jesus is not on the similarity with a reluctant neighbour, but the contrast. "How much more will your Father in heaven...." He says (Lk 11:13). In this conversation as Abraham intercedes for Sodom he is not trying to strike the best deal he can so that evil people can escape the judgment of God.

The clue to a more acceptable understanding comes in Genesis 18:24 "Will you sweep away the righteous with the wicked?" Such an action would contradict the justice of God as Abraham understood it. To destroy fifty righteous people along with the unrighteous in Sodom would simply not be fair. The subsequent conversation is about the justice of God. The number is immaterial, even though Abraham stops at ten. To destroy the righteous along with the unrighteous, the undeserving along with the deserving, is simply unjust. And Abraham, like most of us, cannot attribute to God the kind of behaviour which would be condemned in another human being.

As we read the conversation in this way we discover that what began as pleading intercession for a doomed city quickly becomes a question of God's integrity. The heart of Abraham's argument is to be found in verse 25 "Will not the Judge of all the earth do right?" After all it is by God's righteousness and justice that all other is determined. Our faith, like Abraham's, is built on the integrity of God. If life is not meaningless there must, in the end, be a God who always does the right thing. If He sometimes gets it wrong we are all sunk! We would do well to remember that when we are faced with some of the most difficult questions that come our way. There are no easy answers, but at the heart of our faith is the deep and unshakable conviction that the Judge of all will in the end do the right thing. He, as our story makes abundantly clear, will arrive at his judgments after familiarizing himself with all the facts. Only he knows the whole truth, and so ultimately only God is in a position to pronounce an appropriate verdict. We would do well to avoid taking the place that rightly belongs to Him, and whilst we do need to declare the whole counsel of God when that counsel has been revealed, we avoid speaking for him when our knowledge of complicated situations is, unlike His, only partial.

As a model for prayer, and especially intercessory prayer, we would do well to make a few more observations before leaving this profound story.

God invites Abraham into the conversation. Once again He takes the initiative. He wants us to speak to Him, and to share the things which challenge our faith with Him. This is the last thing many Christians are willing to do. We try and get it sorted out by speaking to everyone else except God about it. Somehow we feel ashamed of our doubts and questions. But God wants us to talk to Him about them.

In such a conversation God wants us to speak as frankly to Him as Abraham did. And why shouldn't we? He knows anyway. We cannot hide our true feelings from Him and this passage, in harmony with the rest of scripture, invites us to express them in prayer to God.

Abraham's prayer was built on what he understood of God's character. He argues on the basis of God's integrity. God cannot deny Himself. He cannot act 'out of character'. It therefore follows that God delights when we ask according to what we know of Him, when we claim His promises, and stake our lives on His very nature.

Seeing things from God's perspective
Genesis 20:1-18

In these studies we are examining the life and faith of Abraham and, since he does not feature in Genesis 19, we are omitting a detailed study of that chapter. It records the destruction of Sodom and Gomorrah, and when the details of the story are examined it is not difficult to understand why God's judgement fell. No doubt the inhabitants of the cities believed they were entirely free to indulge themselves in whatever they fancied without moral constraint. The story brings a timely reminder to every generation that wholesale sin invites wholesale destruction. We cannot sin with impunity. When a society loses its moral framework its days are numbered. Abraham witnessed the destruction of Sodom and Gomorrah and many have witnessed the fall of subsequent kingdoms which ignored the moral law on the grounds of personal freedom. Whether the judgement of God comes by fire and brimstone or by social disintegration is less important than recognizing that no society can survive if it ignores the morality which in itself is an expression of the nature of God.

As Chapter 20 begins we are confronted by a familiar scenario. Abraham the committed pilgrim is moving on and finds himself in Gerar, a border town between Canaan and Egypt and a favourite place for nomads to camp for a while. It was a royal city with Abimelech reigning as King.

Abraham's arrival could not have gone unnoticed. After all he was leading a great tribe of people, animals and servants and there is little doubt that his reputation had gone before him. From Abimelech's point of view this was not just a passing caravan, but the arrival of an embryo nation. Did he see Abraham's arrival as a threat? We do not know, but it is helpful to remind ourselves that often political alliances were cemented by marriage treaties. Maybe that is what motivated Abimelech.

We also need to remember Abraham's previous experience. Did the journey towards Egypt remind Abraham of his last visit to that area? Were old fears resurrected? Maybe, what is clear is that he was obsessed with the thought that the king would want to marry Sarah and once again Abraham would be seen as a threat which had to be eliminated. It had happened before, and the same plan was hatched again; he would say that Sarah was his sister. Far from being the great man of God who never makes a mistake Abraham is revealed with the flaws which are common to us all. He faltered over a relatively small danger, when seen in the great scheme of things, because he was gripped by fear.

At this point it would be helpful to pause and reflect on this incident from different perspectives. From Abraham's point of view his decision was a pragmatic solution to a recurring problem. He could save his own skin by misrepresenting the facts. But from God's point of view the stakes were much higher. God had a strategy for the salvation of the human race. Abraham's role was crucial, but so was Sarah's. What appeared to be a minor matter for Abraham would, from God's perspective, jeopardize the salvation of the world. Sometimes we have no idea how important apparently minor matters can be when seen from God's perspective.

The importance of this matter from God's point of view can be understood from the course of action which He undertook. After Sarah had been incorporated into Abimelech's harem God intervened, both to protect her and to guard his salvation strategy. In a dream He challenges this pagan king by confronting him with the truth. Inadvertently Abimelech had taken another man's wife. He was as good as dead because of it. The intervention provides an insight into the customary morality of the day. Marriage was sacrosanct. To take another man's wife was to place one's life in jeopardy. Fidelity in marriage and chastity outside it have roots which go very deep in the Judeo-Christian tradition. Whilst there is much in the Old Testament which needs careful interpretation in the light of the New Covenant here we see an example of sexual ethics which go back to the very beginning of the covenant people. With this understanding it is easy to see why the sin of Sodom and Gomorrah was so serious.

Further, we must not miss the fact that this standard was required of a king outside the covenant people. This is not just a social convention, but a divine requirement. It is woven into the fabric of the human race and, as Paul reminds us in Romans 1, there is a moral law in the heart of all, by which we will be judged and which every living person has broken. This is not a law imposed by a God in whom we may or may not believe, a law which we may choose not to accept. It is a reflection of the will of our creator and woven into the fabric of human life.

Even though Abimelech had taken Sarah as his wife there had been no sexual relations with her. Abrimelech knew that, and so did God. It would have been inconceivable that Abimelech should lose his life for something he had not done. Interestingly, the dream reveals that his lack of action in this area was the direct result of God's constraining hand upon him. The Almighty had kept him in ways of which he was unaware at the time.

Even though Abimelech was innocent no one else was aware of his innocence. This matter needed to be settled publicly. The truth must come out. Indeed, that truth must also expose the fact that Abraham had acted deceitfully. A confrontation was essential and it took place the following morning. One can only imagine the tension in the meeting. Abimelech was innocent, but appeared guilty. Abraham was guilty, but appeared innocent. Abimelech held the power but Abraham held the moral high ground.

When challenged, Abraham explains his actions. He also seeks to explain his motives. In the alien environment he felt that his life would be threatened, because there was no fear of God in that place. Further, Sarah was his half-sister so it was not a complete lie. Once again, in a completely human way, Abraham tries to justify his actions with a compromised confession. It is less than coming clean, which makes God's continuing gracious covenant all the more wonderful.

From a purely human point of view we can see that both Abimelech and Abraham acted in a way which we understand. Abraham was obsessed by fear and his actions were dictated by pragmatism. Abimelech acted in innocence. But the contrast comes when God challenges them both. Abimelech, who is outside the covenant, seeks to put matters right as soon as he can. Abraham tries to twist the truth to excuse his own guilt. Yet through it all God is gracious and just.

Even through Abraham was to blame and he and Sarah had conspired to deceive; Abimelech is, in the eyes of the people, the guilty party. A public offence required a public gesture to bring the matter to a conclusion. Reparations were offered. Abraham was given a welcome throughout the kingdom and Sarah's reputation remained untarnished.

As the story ends we are told that Abimelech's wife and harem had become barren as a result of Abimelech's action. We may find this difficult to understand, but it is clear that when the root problem was addressed this problem was solved as well. It comes as a reminder that so many human ills do not have a cause which is immediately apparent. But when the root problem is solved the other things are solved as well. How wonderful, therefore, that Abraham prays for Abimelech, and in response to those prayers his essential problem is solved. The story provides just another example of the mess we get into when we try and solve our problems without any reference to God, and how remarkable are the results when God has His way.

Abimelech had been innocent, but appeared guilty. He had to make restitution when in his heart he knew that he ought not to be doing it. Abraham, who had been guilty of deception, came out of it looking clean whilst Abimelech who had been innocent came out of it having lost face and a lot more besides. How often the conduct of those within a covenant relationship with God can be shamed by the conduct of those who do not claim such a relationship.

Isaac is born and a family is divided
Genesis 21:1-21

The chapter opens with the wonderful news that after all those years God kept His promise. Despite Abraham's faltering faith and all the other reasons why, from a human point of view, the child ought not to be born, God keeps His word. How interesting that the writer of Genesis records the incident by emphasizing God's grace to Sarah. Her shame was dealt with and her disbelief conquered. Despite her old age she became pregnant and gave birth to the son Abraham had been promised. As we have learned throughout this whole story, God always keeps His word. The problem from our point of view is that we so often confuse God's delay with God's denial. But when the answer comes after such a long wait, faith is strengthened in ways that it would not have been if the promise had been fulfilled earlier.

Of course, this is all down to the grace of God. Neither Abraham nor Sarah deserved what God did. It was sovereign grace at work, and the fitting response is one of obedience. So Abraham obediently names the child Isaac, as he had been told, and circumcises him on the eighth day. When the command to name him Isaac had been given Sarah had laughed with disbelief, although she had denied it. Now she laughs with joy and knows that everyone who hears about it will join in the rejoicing. God, we might say, had the last laugh!

The child may have been as much as three years old when he was weaned and it was the custom to celebrate the occasion. The celebrations would have been significant on this occasion for every child, but how much more significant they must have been in the case of this child. He was a miracle baby. So a feast was held. One can picture the scene. Isaac would have been the centre of attention. Everyone would be focused on him, whilst in the background, now deprived of the limelight, we see Ishmael. He had been the only child in that family for 14 years and the teenager found it hard to take the fact that his half-brother was now the focus of attention. There is some difficulty in translating the verb at the end of verse 9. In the Hebrew it is a pun on the name 'Isaac'. The NIV follows the AV and RV with 'mocking', whereas the RV margin reminds us that 'playing' is also a legitimate translation. The context, however, convinces us that 'mocking' is right. He began to poke fun at the little child. Anyone who has had teenage children can understand how such a situation could develop.

It's all too much for Sarah. Had there been resentment towards Hagar and Ishmael all those years? Maybe. What is clear is that on this one day the very presence of 'that slave woman and her son' are unbearable. Now that the child Isaac had been born Hagar and Ishmael were, in Sarah's eyes, dispensable. They had to go. Abraham must send them away, and she told him so. They could have a proper family now, and Ishmael could not be part of it, nor could his mother.

Most modern readers have a deal of sympathy with Hagar. She was only a slave after all. She had no rights. She had served her purpose and bore Abraham a son, even though that was a mistake. It seems as though, motivated by Sarah's anger, Abraham is callously avoiding his responsibilities. Maybe this is why Abraham was so distressed. He was on the horns of a dilemma. He could not do justice to both his wife and Hagar and Ishmael. The circumstances may be different, but we may find ourselves in a similar situation. Whatever we do will not be right. So maybe it is good to remind ourselves that God is quite good at working His will out in less than perfect situations! The fact that we cannot get things absolutely right does not mean that God will no longer have anything to do with us or the situations of all those affected by our decisions. It is into this less than perfect situation that God speaks an assuring word.

Even though Sarah's words were spoken in anger, they still represented God's purposes. Abraham should do as Sarah says. Indeed, the split between Abraham, Sarah and Isaac on the one hand and Hagar and Ishmael on the other was God's will for all those involved. God has many ways of making his will clear to us, and this time it was through an angry wife! Our problem so often is that we cannot accept that what is said may be the will of God if we don't like the way He gets the message across. When we turn to the New Testament we begin to see how this aspect of the will of God worked out. In Galatians 4:21-31 Paul presents the readers with an allegory based on this story. It is often lost on modern readers because we do not understand enough about the background. But now we can see it. Bearing in mind all that has gone before, and how Ishmael was born as the result of human reasoning trying to help God out; and how Isaac came along as the result of God's promise fulfilled in the most unlikely circumstances, we find it easy to understand how Paul sees Ishmael as an example of salvation by works and Isaac as an example of salvation by faith.

Yet even though Ishmael was not to be part of the chosen people of God in the way that Isaac was, he was nevertheless still within God's gracious care. God has a purpose for him too. He will make of him a great nation, as he will of Isaac. Hagar and her teenage son are not beyond God's mercy and love. These insights are of great help as we consider the relationship between the chosen people of God and the descendents of Ishmael. Sometimes the fact of God's choice of a particular people is presented as though God had no concern at all for any other people. Nothing could be further from the truth. The descendents of Isaac were chosen to be the way that God would eventually come amongst His people in Jesus, and He was to be the Saviour of the world. The choice of the few was for the benefit of all. Even though the descendents of Ishmael were not chosen for this specific purpose they were not beyond either God's purposes or His care.

Of course, the pain which Abraham must have suffered in facing this dilemma must have been akin to the pain of divorce. He could neither see them again nor make adequate provision for them. But God did what Abraham was unable to do. In Hagar's despair God searches her out. He knew her sufferings, had heard Ishmael's weeping and was not deaf to her prayers. When all seemed lost for this abandoned mother with her teenage son God steps in, provides what they need in that moment and assures them of a future. He would lead them into health and security. God was to be with this lad and work out His purposes for him too.

Hagar's life had been full of trouble, and that not of her making. She was a nobody, a slave, who had been used and was now discarded. There were, no doubt, some happy moments, but even after Ishmael had been born her presence was an embarrassment and source of tension in the family. Now she was discarded, like a nobody who didn't matter to anybody. But she still mattered to God, and so did her son.

The greater part of her trouble had stemmed from Sarah's flawed suggestion and Abraham's willing co-operation in seeking to gain a son by means other than those God intended. It was a lack of faith on his part. He stepped outside the purposes of God and the subsequent years brought untold domestic difficulties to him and considerable pain to others, the most vulnerable people in the story, Hagar and Ishmael. It makes one wonder how our disobedience brings pain to the most vulnerable members of our society. Thank God that despite our disobedience God still remains gracious to all, as he was to Hagar and Ishmael.

A Treaty is established
Genesis 21:22-33

It was in chapter 20 that we learned a lot about Abimelech. He was the King of Gerar and the story of chapter 20, remarkable in many ways, indicates his gracious character. Abraham had been deceitful but it appeared as though he was the one who had been wronged. On the other hand Abimelech had acted in ignorance but, because it seemed as though he had taken Abraham's wife for his own, he had appeared guilty. In the face of such misunderstanding Abimelech had done the gracious thing by making restitution and offering hospitality to Abraham and his people in the land over which Abimelech ruled (20:15).

It seems clear, as our current passage begins, that Abraham and his people were beginning to be seen as a threat to Abimelech and his kingdom. The welcome visitor had become prosperous and his increasing power could easily have become a destabilizing influence. It was no doubt this prosperity which led Abimelech to the conclusion that God was with Abraham in everything he did. So Abimelech, who may still have held in his heart deep hurts from the earlier incident and may have felt threatened by Abraham's increasing influence, realizes that it is important to establish a treaty between them. He takes the initiative and approaches Abraham with a request. He simply wants a fair deal. He had offered hospitality to Abraham and his companions and now that they are established in his land he wants to count on their loyalty rather than live in fear of their increasing power. His words are very significant. He wants Abraham to swear that he will not deal falsely with him, which is precisely what Abraham had done in the earlier incident. Abimelech had showed Abraham kindness. Now he wants that kindness to be reciprocated.

So a treaty is made. Abraham gives his word. The relationship between Abraham and his followers on the one hand and Abimelech and his kingdom on the other is to be clearly understood and formally established. If we read this passage in isolation it seems to be just an account of the way in which the treaty was established. But knowing the story as we do we recognize that it is far more than this. As the two men met each one carried the scars of the earlier encounter. Was Abimelech still carrying the hurt he felt? Was Abraham still carrying the guilt? The treaty is not just about formal relationships between people of different races; it is about the need for, and the way to achieve, real reconciliation. Whether we have done wrong, or wrong has been done against us, we can carry the festering hurt and pain in the heart for many years. It makes all future relationships sour and it poisons the human spirit. Someone needs to make a move if things are to be put right. In this case it was Abimelech. He took the initiative. He had been wronged and had acted graciously. That was alright as long as Abraham was in a subservient position, but when he becomes a possible threat things becomes far less comfortable. Even so, to seek reconciliation is a costly business. We never know how we will be received when we make the first move. Maybe that is why Abimelech took Phicol along with him. We all need a bit of moral support sometimes. The journey to seek understanding from those who have wronged us is one of the most difficult journeys we will ever have to make. But it is an essential journey if the future is not going to be plagued with the guilt and hurts of the past.

Abimelech is a wonderful character. Granted, his actions as a king could be seen as being shrewd and politically expedient. But he is kind and gracious to Abraham. In fact Abimelech's behaviour is exemplary, even through he is not one of the covenant people; whilst Abraham, God's chosen servant, leaves much to be desired. How often is the conduct of Christians shamed by those who make no claims to a personal faith? Yet how gracious God is, that He should choose such an imperfect character as the channel for His grace. It makes us realise that there is hope for us all.

Yet if reconciliation is to be real it has to be thorough. There is little point in trying to wipe the slate clean and begin again whilst we still carry continuing grievances in the heart. That's why Abraham mentions the well. One can almost imagine him thinking "Should I mention the well?" He had a grievance and it was important that this matter be settled also.

Of course, we need to remember how important wells were, as a source of water in so arid an environment. All life depended on a water supply, and often it had to be won at significant cost. Digging a well is a very demanding task. And controlling a well means that you control the population of the whole area. This particular well had been dug by Abraham, but seized by Abimelech's servants. This jeopardized Abraham's livelihood. Of course, if the servant seizes the well you suspect that he has done so on the orders of his king. Had Abimelech been behind this? Was it his way of persuading the visitors who he had invited that they were beginning to outstay their welcome? All these questions and suspicions must have been going through Abraham's mind. So it is important that this matter too is settled.

In the event Abimelech did not know anything about it. He had not heard of it until Abraham raised the matter. And once it was raised it could be dealt with. Here again we have an illustration of the way in which relationships can so easily break down. Something happens and we impute motives which are less than pure on to the other person. They may, in fact, have acted in ignorance, or they may be completely unaware of something which we think they were directly involved in. But the fact that we think the worst of them damages and sometimes kills the relationship.

Here again the matter needs to be put right. Abraham needs the well. Abimelech, if he did not know that his servants had seized it, need to get that matter sorted out too. But how is Abimelech to know that the well really belongs to Abraham, that he dug it? Something needs to be done to demonstrate Abraham's commitment to the truth, at least on this occasion. So he takes sheep, cattle and seven ewe lambs from his flock and gives them to Abimelech. Of course ewe lambs were a valuable commodity. They could breed. But in a sense the value of the lambs is not as important as the gesture. For once Abraham does the gracious thing. He had dug the well. He had lost it. He had been aggrieved. He had thought the worst. But now, after a bold attempt had been made to put past matters straight, Abraham does what is necessary to establish the truth. He knew that if reconciliation is to be real it must be complete, and complete reconciliation is often costly. We cannot be deeply reconciled with another and still carry lingering suspicion and pain in the heart. We all, sooner or later have a price to pay.

The footnote in the NIV reminds us that there is a play on words in calling the place Beersheba. It was the place where an oath was taken, seven lambs were given and a well was opened for business again. The treaty of reconciliation was between Abraham and Abimelech, but it had profound implications for all the people who belonged to their kingdoms and tribes. When the deed is done Abraham and Abimelech part and Abraham plants a tree. It will give shade to all those who come to the well, but it will also continue to reinforce his claim to the site of the well. And most important of all, he worships the Eternal God whose sovereign will is worked out in the complicated relationships of ordinary people. So much of this episode in the story has been about ownership and possession. It is good to remind ourselves as it comes to a close that the well was only Abraham's because God had given him the land. For Abraham, Abimelech and for us all, so much of the tension in relationships results from the self will which regards as our own that which God has graciously provided and loaned to us while we are here.

How could God ask for that?
Genesis 22:1-20

Many of us can think of people who have had a very difficult life, yet the way they have approached their difficulties has made them special people. Indeed, one might almost observe that it was the difficulties which made them the people they are. They have had an opportunity to prove God in the worst times, and discovered His love to be enough. If the worst times had never come their way they may never have made that discovery.

Reading this passage from a 21st century perspective, as we inevitably do, it seems beyond belief that God would really require Abraham to sacrifice his son. Not only does it seem a requirement quite out of keeping with the nature of God, but also it makes nonsense of all the promises which God has made to Abraham so far. How could God require Abraham to kill the only son he has, especially as God had already promised that it is through Isaac that a great nation would come to birth?

It is, therefore, important to make a few observations before we examine the story in some detail. Firstly, if we are to get inside the story, and know its full impact we must try and see things from Abraham's point of view. The problem is that we know how the story ends. God does not eventually require Abraham to sacrifice his son. But of course, Abraham did not know that. We may say that he had misguided ideas, but this is precisely how believers often are. Sometimes we get the strangest ideas about what we think God may require of us. We cannot make sense of what we believe God is calling us to do. Yet the important thing is that, whatever the cost, Abraham was prepared to pay it. It may seem a strange, indeed, an abhorrent idea, but whatever it was Abraham was prepared to be obedient to the voice of God as he understood it. That is what really matters.

The writer makes it clear that God was testing Abraham. As buildings or machinery are today tested for their strength of endurance far above what would normally be expected, so God tested Abraham's faith and, wonderfully, Abraham passed the test. His patience had already been tested over many years. Now in stark contrast to the joy at Isaac's birth, there is the challenge to be obedient when he cannot make sense of what God is calling him to do. Walking away together there is a deep sense that the test is personal. God spoke to him by name. And the very fact that it is so deeply personal makes it an intensely lonely experience. There is no one else there to share the burden on his heart. He was called to sacrifice the only child, promised by God and deeply loved because he was such a gift of grace.

If the traditional sites are the correct ones it was a journey of about 45 miles that Abraham and Isaac and the servants travelled together. Little wonder that it took them three days. One can only speculate about what might have gone through his mind as he made the journey. It is the writer of the Epistle to the Hebrews who helps us by reminding us that since God had made the promise of a great nation through Isaac, and since God had called Abraham to sacrifice his only son, Abraham must have realized that God was able to raise his son from the dead (Heb 11:17-19).

As worship was usually accompanied by animal sacrifice it was quite natural for the boy to enquire where the lamb was for the sacrifice. Everything else was there, wood, fire and knife, but where was the lamb? Could it be that on the journey faith had grown in Abraham's heart? After all, he told the servants "I and the lad will go....we will worship....we will return". Here was no lamb. He knew it was to be his son, but he dared to believe that God would keep the promise onto which Abraham had held for many years. God could not break his word. Even though Abraham could not understand how God would do it he knew that the lad would return with him when the sacrifice was over. The integrity of God depended on it.

Where was Isaac in all this? Was he, as is often supposed, completely passive as the incident unfolds? Could he not have run away when he realized his life was threatened? Or could it be, as some commentators have suggested, that even though he did not understand what was happening he was co-operative with his father's will? That makes his faith as strong, if not stronger than Abraham's. In this, and all aspects of this story we need to balance the test which Abraham was going through with the faith which he had and which he had clearly shared with Isaac. He did expect to sacrifice his own son. He also expected that they would both return.

It was the angel's voice which brought Abraham's dilemma to an end, in the nick of time. The ram caught by its horns was to be the substitute. The death of the ram meant the life of the lad. God had kept his word again. He had provided what was necessary. Such was the impact of the event that the place where it happened was given the name Jehovah-jireh, the Lord will provide.

The test was over and Abraham had passed. His obedience had proved his faith in God, a faith which goes far deeper than his understanding. As a consequence God's promise is renewed and amplified. His descendents will be as numerous as the stars in the sky and the sand on the seashore. We might thankfully observe that generations of people have come into the blessing of God because Abraham kept faith with God and because God kept faith with him. If Abraham is upheld throughout scripture as an example of outstanding faith we might rightly observe that in this story we have a further example of what that faith really is. At its heart there is a trust in God when we cannot understand how His will is going to work out, and an attitude which is prepared to sacrifice whatever is most precious to us that God's perfect will may be fulfilled.

So what is the story really about? Without doubt there are lessons about the nature of faith. Now we know what kind of faith to strive for. But is there something more?

As we began these studies we reflected on the importance of Abraham's life in all subsequent Jewish and Christian faith and devotion. He is the great, outstanding example of faith in the Old Testament. Against all the odds, when to do so seemed irrational, Abraham continued to believe God. He trusted that, even though he could not understand it, God was bound to keep His promises. In the life of Abraham God was laying the foundations of understanding which were to become crucial centuries later, especially in the New Covenant established through the life, death and resurrection of Jesus.

As God tests Abraham in this passage He is once again laying the foundation stones of understanding on which the faith of subsequent generations is to be built. With spiritual hindsight we identify these foundation stones by some of the phrases and words used in this story.

When the puzzled Isaac sees the fire and the wood, but asks his father where is the lamb for sacrifice Abraham replies, "God will provide himself the lamb." How significant the sacrificial lamb became in subsequent Jewish religious understanding. One wonders whether some of the crowds thought of this story when they heard John the Baptist cry out "Behold the Lamb of God" when he caught a glimpse of Jesus on Jordan's banks. We do not know whether they made this crucial identification, but we can. In Christ the assurance of Abraham's heart had found its ultimate fulfilment. God has provided a lamb.

In verses 12 and 16 Isaac is identified as the 'only' son. Of course he was, but what is significant is that when the Septuagint (a Greek version of the Old Testament) was written the translators translated the Hebrew word for 'only' as 'beloved', *agaretos*. This is precisely the word used of Jesus at His baptism and transfiguration.

When we take all these elements of the story together – the promise that God would provide a lamb, the identification of Jesus as the Lamb of God, the way that both Isaac and Jesus are described as the only, beloved, son – and when we remember that the ram which was provided died in the place of Isaac – the harmony of this story with the gospel story seems too strong to be merely coincidental. That is why many people have seen this story as one of the ways in which God tried to prepare the spiritual consciousness of His people for something far more wonderful which He was to do many centuries later. Like Abraham, God was prepared to sacrifice His beloved son, the Lamb of God, and through His sacrifice we can pass from death to life, just as surely as Isaac did.

There is more. The divine name *Jehovah-jireh*, the Lord will provide, has a rich place in Christian faith and devotion. For many thousands of Christians the discovery that God would provide for their every need has been a wonderfully liberating experience. They remind us that the greater includes the lesser. If God provided our greatest need in the atonement offered through the sacrifice of Jesus, we can rely on him to provide our lesser needs as well. Paul reminds us of the same kind of thing in Romans 8:32 "He who did not spare his own Son but gave him up for us all, will he not also give us all things with Him?" This 'faith principle' was proved many times by great Christians like George Muller and Hudson Taylor and in their own quiet way countless Christians can bear witness to God's wonderful daily provision. Of course, this in no blank cheque inviting us to exploit the grace of God for our own ends. But if we live, like Abraham, as obediently as we can, are committed to do God's work in God's way, God will provide for our every need.

The passage which we have studied is like an initial sketch of the Divine Artist. Centuries later the masterpiece would be revealed in the life, death and resurrection of Jesus.

A Pedigree, a death and the funeral arrangements
Genesis 22:20 – 23:20

We do not know who brought the news to Abraham of his brother's family, or precisely why it is included at this point in the unfolding story, but the fact that it is included indicates how important family trees were for the ancient Jewish race and how carefully records were kept. After all, if God was choosing a race and giving them a land, subsequent generations needed to know whether they belonged to that race or not. So detailed records were kept, as indicated by this brief record and the many other genealogies which occur in the Old Testament.

How interesting that there are no such records in the New Testament. With the New Covenant comes the recognition that salvation does not depend on the family into which you were born, but the grace of God shown to all and the trust which each individual has in that grace. Abraham's faith is what saves him. Time and again the prophets were to call a wayward people back to this. To put it bluntly; God has no grandchildren. It does not matter which human family you belong to, as long as you belong to God. Yet the residual error is still to be found in our post-Christian society amongst those who will remind you, particularly when they want you to do them a favour, that their grandmother was a 'big Methodist'! A frightening image!

Nevertheless, we should not dismiss these few verses as irrelevant too quickly. They do help us to put the pieces together and understand the story better. We are reminded that Nahor was Abraham's brother (see Genesis 11:29) and that he had eight sons, one of whom was Bethuel. It was Bethuel who became the father of Rebekah. Maybe the news is included at this point in the story to help us grasp what is coming later. Maybe it was the news that his brother had produced such a family which led Abraham to take the decision recorded in chapter 24 and which, in turn, led to the choice of Rebekah as a bride for Isaac. But more of that later.

In the meantime we must turn to chapter 23 with the record of Sarah's death and the provision of a burial place for her. Death always brings sorrow, and the death of Sarah was no exception.

Abraham and Sarah had been together so long and shared so much. Our study of their lives has revealed something of their joys and sorrows. Now, as a rich and long life comes to an end, Abraham, this giant amongst men, is reduced to tears. It reminds us again that Abraham, and all the great Biblical characters were, at heart, ordinary human beings like us; and that reminder awakens us once again to the possibilities for ordinary lives like ours when placed in the hands of a gracious and powerful God. If that is what God could do with them, human though they were, there is hope for us all.

Chapter 23 opens with a record of Sarah's age at the time of her death. She was 127 years old. The great age of Sarah, and indeed many other Old Testament characters, raises questions in some minds. How and why did they live so long? Did they have a different way to us of recording the passing of the years? Can we really believe the records as they appear in the story?

Of course, all thinking Christians will have to make up their own minds about this issue, but before we dismiss the Biblical record we ought to bear a few things in mind. For one thing, the fact that such great ages are recorded for some suggests that these were the exception and not the rule. Indeed, sometimes the writers remark particularly about the way individuals maintained their strength and abilities despite their great age (see Deut 34:7). They exceeded the normal life expectancy. In broad terms it seems as though the life of the patriarchs was roughly twice as long as most of us can expect. Longevity was, undoubtedly, seen as a blessing from God; an indication that God's favour rested on the person. Further, the fact that God blessed some individuals in this way affords them a position of particular respect in society. Grey hair is not something to be avoided. It is a mark of wisdom and experience affording the person a special standing in their society. It is no accident that when the writer of Revelation records his vision of the exalted Christ he tells us his hair was white as wool (Rev 1:14). Instead of trying to get rid of grey hair we maybe ought to wear it like a crown.

There is evidence from ancient Egypt that they considered the ideal life span to be 110 years. Even today great age is unusual but not unknown. According to a Social Security Administration Report there were 10,700 centenarians in the United States in 1976. In 1638 Thomas Parr was summoned to London by Charles I because church records and other evidence showed him to be 152! By such standards 127 does not seem at all unreasonable. These people may not have had the medical knowledge and techniques which we have today, but they did not have the pollution either. They did not have the life style, the drugs, the intoxicants, the worry and the luxuries which we have; and most of all they had the will and determination to live long enough to allow God's purposes to be fulfilled in them and through them.

Maybe the span of their lives is not as fantastic as once we thought, and maybe it is not unreasonable for us to believe in a God who sustains them in their crucial roles until their work is done. The length of their lives challenges us about the way life ought to be measured. May God grant us all to be sustained long enough to do all that God intends us to do, and then may we graciously pass the torch of faith on to the next in line as they did.

The death of Sarah marked the end of an era and presented Abraham with a particular challenge. He was the head of a tribe, a clan of wandering people. God had promised them a land and they trusted in the promise, but they owned no land. The death of Sarah forces Abraham to obtain some land to serve as a fitting burial place for his late wife. The land was, at this time, occupied by the Hittites and so it was to them that an approach must be made. Throughout this episode in the story it is appropriate to notice the courtesy and respect with which the whole transaction is conducted. The Hittites were not, of course, part of the covenant people; but that does not mean that they are not due the respect which Abraham clearly offers to them. He approaches them with humility, twice bows low before them and without question agrees to the terms they offer. The people of God ought to be distinctive in that they offer courtesy and respect to all, and especially those of different faith and culture.

When approached in such a way the Hittites respond accordingly. Abraham's reputation had obviously gone before him. He is called a prince and one almost feels that they deem it an honour to have been asked. They offer any tomb that he may choose for Sarah.

Abraham knew what he wanted before the request was made. He had already identified a tomb for Sarah. It was the cave of Machpelah set in a field owned by Elphron. Abraham did not know who Elphron was and wanted the Hittite leaders to negotiate with him on Abraham's behalf, but Elphron was sitting in earshot when the request was made. Quickly he volunteers a response. He is willing to give Abraham the cave. No charge will be made.

The footnotes in the NIV indicate that there is some difficulty in accurate translation at this point, although the translation followed by the NIV seems to make more sense of the story in the light of what is to follow. Whilst the cave is offered as a gift Abraham wants the field in which the cave is situated as well. He offers to buy it but Elphron offers to give it to Abraham. After all, what are a field and a cave between a prince like Abraham on the one hand and Elphron on the other? But Abraham will have none of it. He is not going to place himself in a position of moral or financial debt to Elphron. They need to agree a price.

Four hundred shekels of silver seems an exorbitant figure, bearing in mind that the Midianites only paid 20 shekels for Joseph. Maybe Elphron expected to barter for the field, and this was the starting figure. In any event Abraham was having none of it. The solemnity of the circumstances demanded the nature of the transaction. If that was the value of the field, that was the price which must be paid, and so it was. Without further argument the transaction was completed and 400 shekels of silver changed hands. The fact that Abraham could afford such a price clearly indicates the wealth that he had accrued. But it was a price worth paying to provide a resting place for the remains of the one he had loved. As the story concludes we are assured that everything was done correctly and legally. Abraham had gained the field and the tomb. Elphron had become a wealthy man, and Sarah was laid to rest.

Abraham lived in the faith that God would keep His word. God had promised that one day Canaan would belong to Abraham's descendents. He did not own the land, but God had promised. In fact, this field and the tomb in which Sarah was laid were the only pieces of land which Abraham ever owned. As he lays her to rest he is making a statement. He is providing a tomb for his loved one, but he is also leaving her body in a land which his people did not own, but one day they would, because Abraham was sure that God would keep His word.

Finding a wife for Isaac
Genesis 24:1-67

Throughout his long life Abraham had held on to the promise of God that he would be the father of a great nation. Granted, sometimes that faith had been a little shaky, and sometimes he had tried to do God's work for Him, but his faith had been rewarded by the birth of Isaac. God had kept His word. Of course, if the promise was to be fulfilled Isaac in turn needed to have children, and for that he needed a wife, an issue which Abraham addresses in this story.

It was maybe the news Abraham had learned in Genesis 22:20-24 of his brother's family which led him to the decision to find a wife for Isaac from amongst his kinsfolk. He is clearly anxious that Isaac does not go ahead on his own initiative and find a wife from amongst the people of the land in which he is now residing. Abraham knew that the nation which would issue from his family line were to be different from every other people. In a particular sense they were to be the people of God, so here we see what is repeated many times throughout the Old Testament; intermarriage with members of other races, who are not believers, is not acceptable.

The very last verse of the chapter gives us a clear insight into the close relationship which Isaac must have had with his late mother. It is so understandable that after she had waited so long for a son Sarah had a close and special relationship with Isaac. When she died he was obviously lost, and the danger was that needing the love of a good woman Isaac would find his heart stolen by a Canaanite girl. Something must be done. Abraham must protect his son from a danger of which his son is, maybe, unaware.

Abraham's chief servant is summoned and given the task. He is to go to Abraham's brother's family and find a wife for Isaac from amongst them. It says much of the trust which Abraham placed in his servant that he gave him so important a task. The matter was so serious that the servant was bound by an oath to do his best to secure the bride, but if he did his best and still failed it would not be held against him. The practice of placing one's hand under another's thigh when an oath is taken seems to be a practice which is now lost in the shadows of ancient history, although we see it repeated in Genesis 47:29. An action so often needs to accompany a solemn undertaking, and for reasons we do not now know, this action accompanied the making of such a solemn vow.

Daunting though the servant must have found the task, Abraham has learned that God who makes promises enables them to be kept. The hand of providence is on the whole venture and God will provide an angel to enable the task to be completed. With this assurance the servant sets out, taking with him servants, ten camels and choice gifts. It must have been quite a sight. If our knowledge of the sites is accurate the journey was some 400 miles before they all arrived on the outskirts of Nahor. It was evening time and Rebekah, like many other girls was going to the well outside the town to draw water. For her it was just a matter of fulfilling the chores of the day, but it was to be an evening which would change her life for ever.

We are not told the name of the servant who was entrusted with so great a task, but we do know something of his faith. Clearly the faith of Abraham must have rubbed off onto his servant. Abraham had obviously lived up to God's expectation. He had directed his household to keep the way of the Lord (Genesis 18:19). As he arrives at his destination, aware of the difficulties which lie ahead, the servant prays. Note how specific his prayer is. He has enough confidence in the providence of God to ask that in a very specific way he may know which girl is the one chosen to be Isaac's wife. This raises all sorts of questions for Christians today. How can we discern the will of God in specific situations? Is it right to lay conditions before God and expect Him to meet them in answer to our prayers? Many Christians today wish that God's guidance was far more direct than they have experienced. Why is it not so?

Yet behind this situation lay two very important truths which we need to grasp. Firstly, Abraham's servant was sure that God had a will and purpose in his situation. He believed in a personal God who knew the best for his people. There is little chance of us discovering the will of God for our lives if we are not sure that God is bothered what happens to us, or that he is intimately involved with every detail of our lives. Secondly, Abraham's servant was committed to doing God's will when he discovered what it was. That's the point at which so many fail. So often we want to know what God's will is as long as it is in harmony with what we want to do. So often we have a clear idea of what we want to happen, and we ask God to confirm it, or bless our endeavours. What God really wants are people who entirely trust his providential care and are absolutely committed to do his will, whatever the cost.

The prayer was quickly answered. Indeed the answer came before he had finished the prayer, although at this point in the story neither the servant nor Rebekah knew the implications of so ordinary an event. The girl, whom he did not know, seemed to be an answer to prayer, but was she the one? He watched closely to see if she reacted as he had requested in the prayer. Bit by bit the conditions were fulfilled and bit by bit Abraham's servant realized that God was answering his prayer.

There was only one final condition to be met. What race was she? If this girl was to be the one, as it appeared, her pedigree was important. So he asks the question, "Whose daughter are you?" Can you imagine his emotions as she reveals that she is the granddaughter of Abraham's brother. No wonder he bows down and worships. God had brought him through 400 long miles and at the end of the journey God had answered his prayer and revealed his will. In a vast country, populated by a whole range of different ethnic groups, God had led him straight to the one he wanted him to meet.

As we reflect on the story so far it is worth noting what it tells us about the providence and guidance of God. From a human perspective it seems as though Abraham was understandably anxious to find a suitable wife for his son. He comes up with a plan and sends his servant off on this most serious matter. The servant travels 400 miles to find a girl when he is not sure exactly who she is, where she is or what she looks like. He prays and God answers his prayer in a remarkable way. That is wonderful enough. But from another perspective we see that God was involved in the whole thing. Even though Abraham was not aware of it God was stirring the concern in Abraham's heart. God was prompting the prayer of Abraham's servant, so that he asked for what God wanted him to do. Then it all comes together. It is not as though God met them half way, even though that would have been wonderfully gracious. Rather, God inspired, sustained and brought the whole enterprise to a satisfactory conclusion. Maybe this gives us another clue about God's guidance. If we walk close enough to God to have our will lost in his, then he will be in the stirrings of our heart. He will inspire our prayers, even those which we think are expressing our desires. He will motivate, sustain and enable us to do His will, and we will be led to as much rejoicing as was Abraham's servant. It is Paul who reminds us that God "works in you to will and to act according to his good purpose" (Phil 2:13).

From our point of view it would have been rather bold for the servant to ask for overnight accommodation for himself alone, but when you consider the others in the party and the camels as well it really is a tall order! However, the request is made and the welcome offered. Laban greets them as they arrive at Rebekah's home. The camels are unloaded and settled for the night and the supper is prepared. Could it have been the obvious wealth of the unexpected visitor which convinces Laban that here is a friendship worth cultivating? Whatever his motives may have been, it is clear that Abraham's servant is not going to take their hospitality before he tells them the whole story. After all, if things go according to plan he is going to be taking their daughter away. They may never see her again. This matter is too important for an after dinner chat. He needs to tell them the real purpose of his visit.

Step by step the story is recounted and little by little those who hear it recognize that God has been directing the whole operation. You can imagine the atmosphere in that home as the story unfolds. It is truly amazing. In fact it is so amazing that it is obvious that God has been at work. The response too is obvious: "This is from the Lord". However, it does reveal that Nahor's family must have been people who walked close to God as well. Too often God's will is resisted even though it is abundantly plain. How did Nahor's family come to such faith? What had God been doing in their lives during the years since Nahor and Abraham parted? It is one of the great untold stories of the Bible. But even though we do not know the detail we know the result. When confronted with a situation in which God was clearly revealing His will, they could do no other than accept it, "we can say nothing one way or the other". God had made the matter clear. They were committed to doing God's will. It was out of their hands. The matter was settled.

Now Abraham's servant was free to accept their hospitality. They had supper and the servant at least had a good night's sleep, knowing that his mission was almost accomplished. One wonders what kind of a night Rebekah's family had. Maybe it was the result of a restless night that led them to make a natural request. Could she remain for ten days or so, after all they may never meet again? So natural, yet potentially so dangerous. Once God's will is revealed all that remains is for that will to be done. How easy it would have been to change their minds during those ten days. Human nature has a tendency of massaging God's will until it is more palatable. The servant knew that.

He needed to be on his way, mission accomplished.

Whilst the story still holds a sense of wonder for the Western Christian living in the 21st century, it does cause some concern. We marvel at the way God clearly arranged the events which transpired, but we must be careful not to see this story as a Biblical sanction for arranged marriages. It, therefore, comes as something of a relief to read that, at what appears to be a late stage in the unfolding story, Rebekah is consulted. Maybe this consultation was only offered in the hope that Rebekah would insist on remaining at home a little longer. If that was the hope it was ill-founded, for when she was consulted she immediately consents to the servant's plan. What does that say about both her faith and her bravery? Clearly, God had chosen for Isaac a bride of spiritual maturity. The faith which she demonstrated by agreeing to return with Abraham's servant is akin to the faith which Abraham demonstrated when he answered the call of God without any proof that God would keep His word. Isaac was to have a bride whose life was built on the same spiritual foundation as his own. How important that was to be for Isaac and how important it is for us all.

Readers of the NIV will notice from the footnote of verse 63 that there is some uncertainty regarding the exact meaning of the word translated "meditate". We cannot be absolutely sure that this translation is correct, but it is entirely in harmony with the rest of the story. One can picture the scene. Isaac is in the field one evening and as the light began to fade he caught a glimpse of the returning caravan. His heart must have raced. Who knows what Rebekah's heart did? She maintained her modesty and cultural propriety by covering her face. And then the meeting happened. The journey was over, yet for both Isaac and Rebekah, in another sense, it was just about to begin.

There is some significance in the observation that Isaac took Rebekah to his late mother's tent. She was the woman in his life from now on. The marriage took place. Isaac had found a soul-mate, supporter and wife. Rebekah had found a husband. Abraham was able to die knowing that he had done all he could to enable God's promise to be fulfilled. The servant had successfully accomplished his mission. And God's will had been done, through the ordinary which is made miraculous by the providential grace of God.

Gathered to his people
Genesis 25:1-11

It is a rather sobering thought that even though Abraham lived something like 35 years after the marriage of Isaac all that we know about them is recorded in these few short verses. Even for the great men and women of God life is not always full of highs and lows. The highs and lows stand out in history, but there is much that is not worth recording, at least in the view of the historians or the Biblical writers. But that does not mean that God had left Abraham, or that he was out of favour. Life is just like that. We prove our faithfulness, not so much by our endeavours in times of great blessing or great challenge, but in the loyalty of every day life. Abraham must have had dull days as well.

That's worth remembering when we read of other Christians who seem to be always involved in the exciting and memorable things. The danger is that we feel there's something wrong with our spiritual lives if we are not always having some new experience, and some go off here and there after the next one. If our loyalty to Christ depends on our spiritual highs sooner or later we will come to the conclusion that God has left us just because we feel flat. Abraham had his great moments, but he also had many years where nothing happened which is worth recording. But in the ordinary things of every day he still knew what it was to walk with God. What could be better than that?

Maybe we should not assume, just because the record comes at this point in the story, that Abraham did not marry Keturah until after the marriage of Isaac. We know nothing of the precise date. All we know are the names of her children. Some of them and their descendents are going to feature in subsequent history, so they are recorded in the family annals at this point. It will help the following generations know where a whole range of different races and clans originate. It reminds us too that Abraham is the father of many races. The three principal world religions trace their origins back to this Patriarch.

It is always intriguing to meet someone and discover during the conversation that you originate from the same area, or that you know the same people. Jokingly we sometimes say that if we talked long enough we would discover that we are related! It may be truer than we care to imagine. An important part of the Biblical story is the stress on the particular, the things which make the races different from one another; especially the Jewish race. But the other side of that coin, of which we are reminded here, is that there is an inter-relatedness as well. We need to remember that in our quest for reconciliation in a war torn world like ours.

The account seems to suggest that death came to Abraham with some warning. When you get to be 175 it seems reasonable to take the prospect of death seriously. Abraham does so with both justice and prudence. He had a moral responsibility to the sons of his concubines too, so he gives them parting gifts. In a vast land waiting to be populated he seeks to ensure that there is no hostility between family members after his death by ensuring that they live a long way from each other.

When he had set his house in order, acted fairly and given his instructions, Abraham left his considerable wealth to Isaac. He may have fathered many children, but Isaac was heir of the promise of God. He was the one born according to the promise of God and it was through him that the promise would be fulfilled. Abraham's faith had rested on the word of God, but that word needed to be proved not only through the birth of Isaac, but also through his descendents. In leaving Isaac his wealth Abraham was concurring with God's choice. In making his will he sought to act with justice and prudence, but most of all he wanted his actions to be a witness to what God had done and would do.

Funerals often bring families together, and such is the case here. Isaac and Ishmael were united in grief and in performing the last offices of sons for their father. One likes to imagine that in their grief they found a common ground which was deeper than all the family history which had divided them.

When Abraham had bought the grave for Sarah he had ensured that it would accommodate him as well. So he was buried alongside her in the cave at Machpelah. He may have been buried with Sarah but, in a telling phrase, the writer of Genesis reminds us that he was 'gathered to his people'. Even so early in the Biblical story there is a clear belief that death is not the end. There are no details; we will have to wait for that, and no proof. That doesn't arrive until Easter morning. But way back in the history of the human race and the Jewish nation there is a confident anticipation that when death comes it is not the end of us, but a gathering to those who have gone before. Death is the loneliest experience we will ever have to face, because we have to face it alone. Yet after the awful aloneness of death there is the gathering beyond. We believe in 'the communion of saints'.

As a tantalizing footnote to the story, and a trailer for the next, we are told that God blessed Isaac "who lived near Beer Lahai Roi". It is a place we first encountered in chapter 16. There was a well there. It was the place where the frightened Hagar discovered that Abraham's God cared for her too. Is it too bold to suggest that the well, which provided life-giving water for Isaac's family, also served to remind them of the God who would sustain them as He had sustained those who had passed this way before them?

So the story of Abraham, this great man of faith, comes to an end. He is far less than perfect. He trusted God, and then tried to fix things himself on more than one occasion; like we do. Throughout scripture he is held high as an example not of moral perfection or absolute goodness, but because he dared to believe that God would keep His word. Through all the dark years of waiting, in the times when things seemed to be going terribly wrong, when he had no idea how God would do it; yet he dared to believe.

That is what faith is all about. Not feeling, although we thank God for the deep spiritual experiences when they come, but a simple unreserved trust in the integrity of God. God cannot lie. He cannot make a promise and not keep it; not if He is God. That was the great key of understanding which Abraham discovered and which he bequeathed to the world. It was that faith which was 'counted unto him as righteousness'. It is that faith by which we too are saved. Believe! When you have the evidence and when you do not. When the way ahead seems clear though difficult, and when you have no idea how things are going to work out. When you feel great and when you feel terrible. Believe! Dare to believe that the God who kept His promise to Abraham will keep His promise to you too.

Questions to help your study

1. What is the core message of this passage of scripture? Can I sum it up in one short sentence?

2. Have I learned anything new about God the Father, Jesus Christ or the Holy Spirit?

3. What have I learned about myself, about sinful human nature, or about the new nature given to all believers?

4. Is there here any duty for me to observe, any example to follow, any sin to avoid, any promise to lay hold of, any exhortation for my guidance, any prayer which I may echo?

5. How is this passage of scripture useful for teaching me sound doctrine? Does it rebuke me? Does it highlight something which needs correction? Does it help me to become more righteous? (2 Tim 3:16)

6. What does this passage teach me about the nature of the gospel?

7. Is there a key verse or short passage which sums up the message?

8. If I am to be a doer and not just a hearer of the word how must I let the message of this passage shape my understanding, change my attitude, and mould my behaviour?

9. Is there a verse or phrase in this passage through which I have sensed God speaking directly to me and my situation from His word?

10. In what ways should I expect the truths contained in this passage to deepen my relationship with God?

HEADWAY

Evangelical Methodists in prayer and action

The aims of the movement are...

- The promotion of the renewal and revival of the work, worship, and witness of the Church, particularly within Methodism, through prayer and in the power of the Holy Spirit.
- The encouragement of prayer for revival at a personal level, and in the church at home and overseas.
- The furtherance of informed theological discussion in the Church.
- The furtherance of thinking and action on ethical and social issues in a responsible and compassionate way, based on the belief that the righteous will of God must be expressed in the life of society.
- The promotion of joint action with evangelical Christians in all denominations of the Church in local and national events.
- The promotion of mature Christian spirituality in the lives of all members of the Church.

Our basis of faith is that of the Evangelical Alliance, with a specific commitment to the Methodist understanding of salvation, as set out in the 'Four Alls':

- All people need to be saved
- All people can be saved
- All people can know themselves to be saved
- All people can be saved to the uttermost

Membership of HEADWAY is open to any member of the Methodist Church who is in sympathy with the aims and basis of the movement. Associate membership is open to those who are not members of the Methodist Church. Membership information from:

Mrs Hazel Harwood
1 Linden Avenue, Woodseats
Sheffield S8 0GA